The Ultimate Guide to Selling Your Original World Language Resources

Anyone can open an online curriculum store, but how many know how to do it effectively and in a way that maximizes earning potential? Based on years of experience, research, pitfalls, and triumphs, this essential guidebook supports the World Language teacher-author in navigating the exciting world of selling curriculum on an online platform.

With this guide, there is no more sifting through boring content, trying to figure out how it translates to your content area, as the World Language-specific examples in Section 1 (Opening Your Store), Section 2 (Filling Your Store), and Section 3 (Growing a Successful Store) cut to the chase with real-world examples for language teachers. Each section provides critical tips, all designed to boost sales. The guided workspace pages organize planning and content strategies and serve as markers for your store's growth.

Whether you are just starting out or already have a store established, this guide is the #1 tool to "level up" your online curriculum store. If you are a World Language teacher who enjoys making money while you sleep, this is for you!

Erin E. H. Austin is a National Board Certified French teacher in Colorado. She began her teaching career in Minnesota in 2002, and she holds a B.A. in both French and Art Education, an M.A. in Curriculum & Instruction, and graduate certificates in French Studies and Gifted, Creative & Talented Education. She was an NEA Foundation Global Fellow in 2018. She has been an active online curriculum seller since 2014.

Also Available from Routledge Eye on Education

Leading Your World Language Program: Strategies for Design and Supervision, Even If You Don't Speak the Language!
Catherine Ritz

An Educator's Guide to Dual Language Instruction: Increasing Achievement and Global Competence, K-12
Gayle Westerberg and Leslie Davison

Differentiated Instruction: A Guide for World Language Teachers
Deborah Blaz

The World Language Teacher's Guide to Active Learning: Strategies and Activities for Increasing Student Engagement
Deborah Blaz

Using Reading to Teach a World Language: Strategies and Activities
Donna Spangler and John Alex Mazzante

The Ultimate Guide to Selling Your Original World Language Resources

How to Open, Fill, and Grow a Successful Online Curriculum Store

Erin E. H. Austin

Routledge
Taylor & Francis Group

NEW YORK AND LONDON

First published 2021
by Routledge
605 Third Avenue, New York, NY 10158

and by Routledge
2 Park Square, Milton Park, Abingdon, Oxon, OX14 4RN

Routledge is an imprint of the Taylor & Francis Group, an informa business

Library of Congress Cataloging-in-Publication Data
Names: Austin, Erin E. H., author.
Title: The ultimate guide to selling your original world language resources: how to open, fill, and grow a successful online curriculum store /
Erin E. H. Austin.
Description: New York : Routledge, 2021. |
Series: Routledge Eye On Education |
Identifiers: LCCN 2021001535 (print) | LCCN 2021001536 (ebook) |
ISBN 9780367761172 (hardback) | ISBN 9780367748296 (paperback) |
ISBN 9781003165576 (ebook)
Subjects: LCSH: Education, Higher–Marketing–Technological innovations. |
Education, Higher–Computer-assisted instruction. | Language and
languages–Study and teaching–Technological innovations.
Classification: LCC LB2847 .A97 2021 (print) | LCC LB2847 (ebook) |
DDC 371.20068/8–dc23
LC record available at https://lccn.loc.gov/2021001535
LC ebook record available at https://lccn.loc.gov/2021001536

ISBN: 978-0-367-76117-2 (hbk)
ISBN: 978-0-367-74829-6 (pbk)
ISBN: 978-1-003-16557-6 (ebk)

Typeset in Palatino
by Deanta Global Publishing Services, Chennai, India

For B.G.,
the best TpT teammate I could ask for

Contents

Acknowledgments

I owe a huge thanks to my family! My incredibly patient husband, Daryl, kept our house together, kept me (mostly) sane, and picked up the slack while I worked on this "Pandemic Project." And thank you to our kids and dog who, miraculously, didn't destroy the house (or each other) during my writing process, thus affording me more brain space to write.

I am so grateful to my kids' daycare provider, Jana. She provided exceptional care (far more patiently than I could provide!) to my two kids while I stuck myself in front of a computer to write.

I am forever indebted to my content consultant, Elizabeth. I needed someone who knew the ins and outs of TpT to help steer me through this book, and she gave me the information, encouragement, and expertise I needed. She has the unique ability to see the big picture yet give advice on the details at the same time.

My first copy editor, Jane, has encyclopedic knowledge of all things related to the English language. As a language teacher, I like linguistic minutiae, but this woman lives it. I couldn't have done this without her.

Thank you to my photographer, Mina, and my photo stylist, Shelley. Together they helped me look my best for my "adult senior pictures." You guys rock!

About the Author

Erin E. H. Austin is a National Board Certified French teacher in Colorado. She began her teaching career in Minnesota in 2002, and she holds a B.A. in both French and Art Education, an M.A. in Curriculum & Instruction, and graduate certificates in French Studies and Gifted, Creative & Talented Education. She was the 2013 Metro Area Big Sister of the Year with Big Brothers Big Sisters of the Twin Cities, and she now serves on the Associate Board of Big Brothers Big Sisters of Colorado. In 2018, Ms. Austin was  an NEA Foundation Global Fellow, which was the catalyst for her professional interest in Global Education and afforded the opportunity to be a contributing author in Dr. Fernando Reimer's book *Twelve Lessons to Open Classrooms and Minds to the World*. She has been an active online curriculum seller since 2014. The Side Hustle School podcast featured Ms. Austin's TpT work on episode 142. Although she loves living in beautiful Colorado with her family, she is constantly dreaming of her next trip abroad.

Introduction

TeachersPayTeachers.com (TpT) is an online marketplace where teachers from anywhere in the world can buy, sell, and download resources. Think: Etsy for curriculum! It also just happens to be one of the top and fastest-growing ways for teachers to make supplemental—and largely passive—income since its start in 2006.

But since you're here, chances are, you already knew that!

Let me be clear about this book right off the bat: it is not about technology. It's not about what buttons to click and where they're located, nor does it include what a PDF file is or how to create one from a Word document. Though there is *some* of that, it is very little of this book's content. I make the assumption that the teachers using this workbook have a basic knowledge of technology or, at the very least, a good "tech guy/gal" in their work or social worlds to whom they can pose those essential questions.

And because it's not about technology, the information in this book is less about TpT (which I use), and more applicable to *any* online platform for curriculum sales by teacher-authors. TpT is the industry leader, but other companies are vying for their spot in the marketplace as well. The UK-based company Tes is one such platform that many teachers use, and most recently, Amazon is venturing into the waters as well.

This book strives to be evergreen. By that, I mean that the principles presented here change very little over time or platform. Technology, as we know, is ever evolving! But the principles behind opening, filling, and growing a successful online curriculum store are much steadier, *and* they are platform-*independent*.

The information I give in these pages, combined with the workspace sections, is meant to help teacher-authors do one thing: make money off the original resources they create!

I started my teaching career in 2002, and beyond a shadow of a doubt, I have worked with some of the most intelligent, creative, and talented teachers out there. I think about these past and present colleagues all the time, and I wish that all students could have access to the master lessons these teachers create on a daily basis. TpT and related platforms allow this wish to come a few steps closer to reality, and they simultaneously give financial recognition to the creative efforts of such teachers.

I divided this book into three sections: Opening Your Store, Filling Your Store, and Growing a Successful Store. The first section is all about getting your store set up. It serves as the outline for your store/business. The second section requires you to dig deep with the curriculum you create, and it shows how you have a lot more to create and sell than you might initially think. The third section gives you ideas to take it to the next level once you've found a nice rhythm in your online store.

The amount of time you spend in each section is completely up to you, but the faster you work, the sooner you'll make money. A manageable place to start might be 15 months: a 3-month summer to start things off, a 9-month school-year to fill your store, and another 3-month summer to kick it into high gear. Whatever your pace, the book will be here for you, and the workspace pages will have your notes when you're ready to come back to them.

My goal is to help other teacher-authors make a rewarding income off their own imagination and expertise. Selling curriculum I create has changed my work/life world for the better, and I know it can for you too! "But aren't you creating competition for yourself just by writing this?" you might wonder. Maybe, maybe not...but even if I am, I'm not particularly bothered. I don't believe the marketplace for innovative, practical, and clear materials for students is finite at all. As long as we each approach our store and business ethically, there is room for all of us to succeed together!

Lastly, I'm so excited for you! You're attacking a process that can help supplement your income to pay bills and attack debt, but hopefully also to do fun things like take a trip or make a home improvement. And maybe more importantly, you're putting the best of your best curriculum out there for other teachers to use and learn from. Students will benefit from your expertise.

Good luck, and I can't wait to see what outstanding curriculum you share online!

SECTION 1
Opening Your Store

1

The Sky's the Limit

Defining What's Possible

I dabbled around on the TpT website prior to 2014, but that year marks my start of diving into being a serious, albeit part-time, seller. I made the conscious decision to upload eligible resources I created and to put time and energy into earning income from my work.

I liked the idea of making money while I slept—such a foreign concept for a teacher—and I set a goal of paying for the bulk of my honeymoon to New Zealand and Tahiti with TpT earnings. That was my initial motivation, and it proved successful, but there is a myriad of reasons why teachers choose to sell on curriculum selling platforms. Here are a few of the more finacially-based reasons:

- ◆ **Make passive income.** We're living in the Age of the Side Hustle, and passive income hustles are key in the diversification of income streams.
- ◆ **Quit your job.** Don't love your job? Need to be home with your kids? Out of work because of a medical issue? Online curriculum platforms allow teachers to make an income while not in a traditional teaching setting.
- ◆ **Become location-independent.** As a World Language teacher, income from selling curriculum can afford us the

opportunity to live abroad in an immersive language setting, yet still get paid in our home country.

◆ **Take a vacation.** Side income based largely on work we
already know how to do (i.e., create curriculum) is easy to
put into that "fun money" category in the budget.

◆ **Grow a following.** Your curriculum sales can help you
establish a following to attend your sessions at conferences, grow your blog, or increase your social media followers, all of which can (indirectly) lead to more revenue.

No matter what your reason is for selling, be open to the idea
that the reason you *start* selling might not be the reason you *keep*
selling. And no matter your motivation, there is one rule I have
found to be true in every instance and for every seller:

> *Golden Rule for selling curriculum online:*
> *it's a numbers game.*

What does that mean? It means that the more you upload,
the more you make. It's as simple as that. Absolutely keep this
Golden Rule in your head at *all* times. (I won't let you forget
it either because it'll come up in this workbook over and over
again!)

WORKSPACE

What are your financial goals as a curriculum seller? Why are you doing this? If everything went according to plan, what would happen?

Note: These will change! Later on, we'll discuss the difference between two different types of goals, but for now, this is a space for you to jot down some of your initial thoughts and goals.

· --
· --
· --
· --
· --
· --
· --
· --
· --
· --
· --
· --
· --
· --
· --
· --
· --
· --
· --
· --
· --

2

Why Bother?

Making the Case for Selling Curriculum

So, you get it: you can make good money selling curriculum online. Great. But why bother? Can't all of those benefits happen without writing and selling curriculum? Well, yes. You can make passive income by writing a book. You can quit your job if you win the lottery. You can become location-independent simply by teaching online instead of in a brick-and-mortar school. You can afford a vacation with the money you make driving for Lyft, and you can increase your social media following by doing any number of things, both risqué and mundane.

So why, then, is creating an online curriculum store in our best interest? What would make a teacher want to do this instead of getting a job folding clothes all evening and weekend at a local retail store?

To answer that, I'm going to assume a few things. First, I'm going to assume that the reason you're an educator is because it's your calling. You can't, in fact, imagine doing anything else with your life and being as fulfilled, despite the fact that teaching is *hard*. I will also assume that you love your students—maybe not *every* student *all the time*, but for the most part, you love your students and get joy from teaching. Lastly, I am also going to assume that you want to become a better teacher.

If my assumptions are true, a better question might be: why would you do anything *other than* write and sell original curriculum? Creating an online curriculum store is work, to be sure, but the professional benefits are real:

- ◆ **It enhances your résumé.** Establishing a presence as a curriculum seller contributes to your expertise in your field. When you move and start job hunting, or when you're searching for your next professional step, it won't hurt to show the interview committee that your non-school time is still spent contributing to the field of education.
- ◆ **It allows you to quit that "other" job.** When you make money selling curriculum, you can give up waitressing, summer landscaping work, or whatever else you happen to do for income. Now you can have a side job that complements your daytime career, a job for which you were professionally trained.
- ◆ **It forces you to improve your craft.** The products that you create and sell will be reviewed by your buyers. Your organization, teaching skills, and clarity of message *must* be on point. If they're not, you'll get called out in the reviews. It typically only a takes a couple of negative reviews before a seller realizes that they have to step up their game, and he or she makes appropriate changes.
- ◆ **It sharpens your language skills.** Not only does writing curriculum to sell online improve how you create curriculum, but for World Language teachers, it improves our *language skills*. In creating products, we talk to native speakers ("Hey, am I using this correctly?"), we get increasingly familiar with verb forms (*500 Verbs* books are our friends), and we constantly consult grammar manuals to gain clarity on usage and exceptions. The language input we get from our research plus the (correct) language output we use in our resources leads to overall improvement in our skills.
- ◆ **It changes the landscape of classroom resources for everyone.** Online curriculum store platforms are revolutionizing the market for World Language teacher resources. It used to be that there were only a few, select catalogs from which to buy resources, and after

we bought them, what if they weren't what we thought they were? What if they were full of errors? (We used *Wite-Out*, that's what!) The money we spent on that resource is long gone. But with online resource platforms, we have access to a lot more information before we purchase goods for our classroom, and we can also read what other teachers who have bought the product before us thought of it. When we contribute to this marketplace, we contribute to making better resources more accessible for teachers.

◆ **It benefits students.** This is, arguably, the most important professional benefit to selling your original curriculum. We've all had those activities that we created and that made us think, "Man, this is great stuff! I really hit it out of the park with this! The students are really getting it now!" Don't *all* students—not just *your* students—deserve access to the best products out there? Of course they do. And you can be an important factor in all students receiving the best education possible.

◆ **It benefits teachers.** If you created a well-designed resource that helps students, inevitably, it will help their teachers. All teachers love it when we have a tool that helps kids, and I've never met one teacher who cares if they created the resource or if it came from someone else. If it's best for kids, we want it, we will use it, and we'll keep coming back to the place where we found it.

An argument here might be that you like working at a restaurant or in a downtown retail shop after school because it allows you time *away* from your job; it's relatively mindless work, and writing/selling curriculum just doesn't allow you to turn your brain off. I get that. But I would counter that putting on awesome music, reading a page-turner book, cooking a tasty meal, working out outdoors, and any number of other healthy activities all can be equally as effective at helping us unwind from the school day. Might it be better to use your professional educator skills to generate income while using hobbies to give your mind downtime and rejuvenation? It's worth considering.

3

Why Me?

Knowing Your Worth

Opening an online curriculum seller account and getting started can be so much fun! But after the initial excitement, don't be surprised if fear and anxiety set in, potentially with a smattering of self-doubt, just for fun. *Who am I to sell what I create? What do I know? Is this worth my time? Should I even be trying this? What if I get a bad review on a product?*

Who are you to sell? You're an education professional, period. More than likely, you have training, on-the-job experience, and a degree (or multiple!) verifying that to be true. If you are a veteran teacher, you undoubtedly have mastered at least some aspects of your job that you can share and for which you can be financially compensated. You have a solid understanding of what works well with kids and what doesn't. You've "been there, done that," and you've adjusted your craft accordingly. You've had experience with multiple educational tools, systems, programs, texts, and fads, all of which you can use to your advantage. If you are relatively new to the profession, you're fresh! You have fresh ideas that are new and cutting-edge. You might have a comfort with certain technologies (e.g., apps, templates, online platforms) that other teachers don't have. Best of all, you have an energy and enthusiasm that veteran teachers would do well to have a dose of!

What do you know? You know your content, your students, your grade level, your specific online platform, and you know your *language*. But let's get over one major roadblock specific to World Language teachers: native speakers versus non-native speakers. Not being a native speaker is not a good enough reason to not open a store and sell your best work. (Read that sentence again.) Too many language teachers are completely self-conscious about their work because they aren't native speakers.

On the one hand, I do understand because I am not a native speaker. But on the other (larger?) hand, thinking that what you create isn't as good as a native speaker's materials simply has no basis in reality. All you have to do is take a quick look at social media to have this point proved. How many native speakers of English routinely mix up possessives and plurals? (Holiday cards are a major culprit!) Or how many native speakers *still* don't know the difference between there, their, and they're? Lose and loose? Effect and affect?

Furthermore, technical language skills are one (small, in my opinion) aspect of teaching. Consider native speakers of English teaching English classes, for example. Does their native language mean they have an innate ability to reach kids? Or to create worthwhile curriculum that resonates with their learners? Not at all. Being a native speaker likely means you have a gorgeous, clean accent. No argument there. But there is no reason to think that a native speaker's language or teaching ability is flawless.

Is this worth your time? Well, that depends. What do you want your life to look like? What's your lifestyle, and how much money do you need to maintain that? There are absolutely people out there who earn a living equivalent to or greater than their teaching salary by selling resources online. How would that change your life if that were you?

Should you even try this? I understand having a fear of the unknown, but consider the risks versus the rewards. If you select a Basic Account, there is literally no financial risk at all, and if you select a Premium Account the financial risk is less than $100 (see the next chapter for specifics). Timewise, there is a risk; you will undoubtedly have to donate time to this endeavor. But each potential seller needs to ask him/herself if the possible financial rewards are worth that time. If you're a math nerd (in the best way possible), do the math! How much would you have to earn on a monthly basis to earn minimum wage (as a starting point) for the hours you put in? Or how much would equal *double* minimum wage? Then try out selling for a year. Just one year. Did you hit your mathematical mark?

Furthermore, take yourself out of the equation as the "unsure one." What if one of your students came to you and talked to you about an opportunity that they weren't sure about. You see that there is some risk involved, though not a lot, and you know that your student has qualifications that would make him/her excel in their chosen realm. What would you say? Would you tell your student, "Hmm…I'm not sure about this. Maybe you shouldn't try it?" Or would you say, "Heck, yes! Go for it! What have you got to lose?" If you wouldn't sell another person short or discourage them, don't do it to yourself.

What about negative reviews? Here's a spoiler alert: you *will* get a bad review. (Multiple, actually.) There's no way to please everyone, and we deal with this as teachers every year. We'd be naïve to think that every student and every parent we ever encounter gives glowing reviews to other students and parents about our teaching skills, our knowledge, or even our personality. Somehow, we still go into the profession. I challenge you to approach selling original resources with a similar attitude.

The point is this: you don't have to be National Teacher of the Year to have a successful curriculum store. You just have to believe in the effectiveness of your materials on educating kids.

WORKSPACE

What are your strengths as a teacher? What are your qualifications? What do you bring to the table?

Note: this isn't about selling curriculum, this is just about *teaching*. Write down a strength for each bullet point here. Never, ever, sell yourself short.

- --
- --
- --
- --
- --
- --
- --
- --
- --
- --
- --
- --
- --
- --
- --
- --
- --
- --

4

To Pay or Not to Pay?

Selecting a Status

When you decide to join a curriculum selling platform, you will likely have different options, or "levels," for your account. If you choose to sell with TpT (with the *Join Us* link on the TpT website), you have two options: the Basic Seller Account and the Premium Seller Account.

When I first started out, I began with a free account. I thought, "Once my earnings hit $59.95 in a single month, that'll be my cue to switch to Premium." (Switching, by the way, is quite simple.) That worked for me at the time, but it was admittedly arbitrary and not mathematically sound.

There is nothing wrong with trying out a Basic Account, but if your finances allow, go all in with a Premium Account right away. There are two reasons for this. First, it allows you to make more money right away. There is a significant difference between a 55% and an 80% teacher-author cut on earnings, not to mention the transaction fees that are automatic with the Basic Account. Making more money is certainly an incentive to keep going! Second, we're wired to "get what we paid for" when we purchase a service, product, or membership. With the Basic Account, it's too easy to be ho-hum about our progress; with the Premium Account, we have an incentive to make this work because we want to make it worth our investment.

TABLE 4.1

Basic Seller		Premium Seller	
Pros	Cons	Pros	Cons
◆ Free ◆ Unlimited uploads ◆ Can participate in TpT School Access	◆ Earnings payout is 55% of your sales ◆ Transaction fee ($0.30 per resource) ◆ File sizes are limited to 200MB ◆ Does not allow video uploads	◆ Unlimited uploads ◆ Earnings payout is 80% of your sales ◆ Transaction fee is less ($0.15 per resource, only if total order is less than $3) ◆ Accepts file sizes up to 1GB ◆ Allows video uploads ◆ Access to premium features ◆ Can participate in TpT School Access	◆ $59.95/year (as of this publication)

5

Branding Yourself

Choosing the Right Store Name and Image

Today we hear near-constant messages about branding. *What's your brand? You need to build your brand. Social media is part of your brand.* It's a bit overwhelming, especially when we are teachers, not marketing professionals.

When deciding on a store name, start by hunting around. Check out other TpT sellers—particularly those in World Language—and see what they call their stores. Look for inspiration. And while you're at it, relax! You can easily change your store name at any point. After five years with one name, I changed mine, and I saw no negative repercussions.

When I opened my store, I found it easiest to sort through the names I *didn't* want first. I didn't want my actual name to be part of it because I wanted to preserve some amount of anonymity. I also didn't like names in the genre of "Teacher, Mommy, Wife" because, full disclosure, that's just way too much cheese. (And that's saying a lot for someone who was born and raised in Wisconsin!) I wanted a name that was professional, yet original.

It's also important to consider *creativity* versus *clarity*. For example, maybe you want to name your store the *Blue Sky Boutique* after a particularly poignant allusion in a poem you read in an undergrad Spanish Literature class. Is it creative? Yes. Is it meaningful? Yes, to you. Is it clear? No. You might be a Spanish teacher, but that store name could just as easily be for a store that sells math resources to first-grade teachers. This may or may not bother you, but it's something to consider.

As a World Language teacher, there's the question of whether or not to put the store name in English or in your target language. I don't think there is a problem with either, and I've seen memorable store names in both categories. I would, however, caution against using a store name that includes an accent. These can pose problems later when/if you branch off and add to your passive income stream and brand. (More on that in Section 3.)

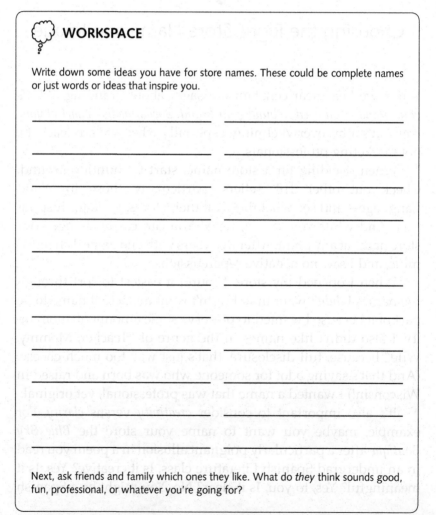

WORKSPACE

Write down some ideas you have for store names. These could be complete names or just words or ideas that inspire you.

_____   _____

_____   _____

_____   _____

_____   _____

_____   _____

_____   _____

_____   _____

_____   _____

_____   _____

Next, ask friends and family which ones they like. What do _they_ think sounds good, fun, professional, or whatever you're going for?

Store Name + Logo

=

The Start of Your Brand

Next up is your store image. Just like the store name, the image can be easily changed, and it's productive to hunt around and get ideas from other sellers first. What stands out to you as cool-looking? What *don't* you like?

In the beginning, I used a picture of myself standing on a mountain in France doing a yoga pose. It was meaningful to me because that mountain was the subject of many Cézanne paintings (I'm dual-certified in K–12 French and Art), and I'm a yoga instructor. The photo was also taken from behind, which I liked, again for anonymity purposes. But basically, I used that photo because it was what I had.

You, too, may opt for *just a photo you have*, and there are many people who use the classic "school picture" for their store photo. But if you're thinking about a logo instead of a photo, know that it doesn't have to be expensive. Here are some ideas:

◆ **Word art.** You might just want a store name in a fun font! There is absolutely something to be said for simplicity. (Note: make sure you use a font that is labeled for commercial use.)

◆ **Avatars.** Plenty of education resource stores use avatars as an image. (Again, check the commercial use rights on the avatar-building site you use.)

◆ **Graphic design.** Hiring and finding a graphic designer doesn't need to be expensive. There are plenty of artists on sites like fiverr.com who are trying to build their résumés and will design a logo for a very low cost.

◆ **Your network.** Who is in your network? Do you know anyone with computer and/or art skills? Does the art teacher in your school do graphic design? When I moved from a photo to a logo, I was able to do so because the Digital Design class at my school used my store as a project. I was invited to talk to the class about my TpT store, and the students asked (very professional!)

questions. A couple weeks later, I had 20+ designs to choose from!

If you're using an *image* (photograph, avatar, etc.) instead of *words*, there is more to consider. Depending on the image you use, you might be giving away information that you don't want to give. (Or maybe you do!) Do you want buyers to know your sex, race, and body type, for example? Some sellers prefer to keep everything about their stores neutral so as to maintain anonymity and ward off any *potential* issues because of any of those factors. Other sellers know without a doubt that they want buyers to know they're a person of color, for example. What you want may change as your earnings from your store grow as well. There is no right answer here; there is only what is right for *you*. But this is definitely a component to your marketing strategy.

To a lesser extent, your email is also part of your brand, and you need an email address attached to your seller account. I recommend setting up a new Gmail account with your store name. This will help keep personal and business communication separate. You should use your store name in your address (another reason not to use foreign characters/accents in your store name), and most email services have a spot for you to upload your logo/ store image as well.

6

Shift Your Lens

Sorting What You Have and Don't Have (Yet)

Now let's talk about your original materials—the main event! Some teachers are dissuaded from opening an online curriculum store because they (mistakenly) think that what they create isn't "fancy" enough. When I think about all of my current and former colleagues, I can count the ones who make "fancy" lessons, handouts, and projects on the one hand. I'd be counting to a pretty high number, though, if I counted the number of colleagues who created fantastic, educationally relevant, clear, and/or creative materials.

The following workspace is a list of materials that I either sell in my store or items that are related to having a store, as well as a list of what I *don't* have. My point is to show that what I sell—and am successful with—is pretty simple. In fact, there are likely things you have that I don't and things you can create that I can't.

Equally as important as thinking through what you *do* have and what you *could* have is considering those "hidden" items. By that, I mean those items that we can and do easily create but that we've never considered selling. See Table 6.2 for examples.

You may look at some of the items in the second column of Table 6.2 and think, "What? People would buy that?" Yes, they would; and yes, they absolutely *do*. Some of my most frequent sales are items that I nearly didn't upload because I didn't think anyone would buy them.

WORKSPACE

Go through this list with three highlighters:
green = what you have
yellow = what you might not currently have, but that you could easily have
pink = what you don't have
Feel free to add any others you thought of as well!

What I have/do	What I don't have/do (yet!)
◆ Word documents	◆ Video
◆ PDFs	◆ Google docs
◆ PowerPoint files	◆ SMART board activities
◆ Items for multiple classes	◆ A massive pool of potential
◆ Items for another subject I teach	buyers (Spanish teachers probably
◆ Assessments	have the biggest pool of potential
◆ Projects	buyers)
◆ Game	◆ Excel documents
◆ Activities	◆ An LLC
◆ Bundles	◆ "Cute" documents and covers
◆ Periodic platform sales	(You've seen these all over
◆ Low (too low?) price points	TpT...documents that look made
◆ A strong desire to make passive	by a corporation because of all
income	the special fonts and clip art)
◆ An Intellectual Property (IP)	◆ Actively pursue followers on the
lawyer	platform
◆ A blog	◆ Professional Development (PD)
	documents (e.g., outline for
	teaching a PD session on a given
	topic)
	◆ Committee documents (e.g.,
	Wellness Committee ideas)
	◆ YouTube Channel
	◆ Create for an entirely different
	grade level than I teach
	◆ Purchase fonts
	◆ Purchase clip art
	◆ A huge social media presence

TABLE 6.2

OBVIOUS TO SELL	BUT WHAT ABOUT...?
◆ Assessments (quizzes/tests) ◆ Worksheets ◆ Games ◆ Activities ◆ Projects ◆ Introductory handouts	◆ Templates ◆ Graphic organizers ◆ Rubrics ◆ Lists (e.g., discussion topics, journal topics) ◆ Outlines/timelines (e.g., yearly outline of units and pacing for AP German) ◆ Ideas for different school committees ◆ Non-teaching-related items (e.g., book club guides, baby/wedding shower games) ◆ "How To" documents

When you consider what you have to sell, you may find it useful to refer back to the workspace section on your strengths. Make sure that you keep your strengths in the forefront, because resources related to your strengths are likely what are going to bring in the most sales.

Another place you can go to for ideas is your curriculum selling platform itself. When you upload a document, you have to select the type of resource that you're selling, and there's a lengthy list. If you need inspiration, it can be useful to go through that list to see what some other possibilities are. Chances are good that you'll see something that sparks your interest *and* your talent!

After sorting out what you have, what you could have, and what your "hidden items" are, there's one more key piece. Up to this point, we've only discussed what *you* want to *sell*. The flip side of that coin is asking yourself what *other teachers* want to *buy*. These two lists are not going to 100% align. Do you see what that means? It means that if you create for your own wants and needs *as well as* others' wants and needs, you suddenly have a much bigger sales potential!

Shift Your Lens:

*1. It's about what you **have** and what you **could have.***
*2. It's about what's **obvious** and what's **hidden.***
*3. It's about what you want to **sell** and what others want to **buy.***

7

Different People, Different Needs

Knowing Your Buyers

One of the biggest mistakes online curriculum sellers make when opening a store is going into it with the assumption that our buyers are just like us. If you're serious about making money from your original resources, it is essential to expand your view right from the get-go. Remember the Curriculum Seller's Golden Rule: *It's a numbers game.* Creating for more than one type of buyer/ teacher equals more sales.

Think of it like this: in the classroom, every good teacher knows that they have to teach concepts in a variety of ways because every student they meet learns a little bit differently. It's the same with curriculum buyers. They're all coming to your store for a different reason, looking for something a little bit different. For example, *you* might exclusively teach a Comprehensible Input (CI) method, but guess what? Not everyone is looking for CI materials. Some are, but if you can create non-CI materials as well, why not do it?

It's also usually during this "thinking about your buyers" phase that self-doubt starts to creep in yet again. *Who am I to sell? What do I know? Anybody could make the things that I'm selling.*

I'm going to be stern here: STOP. Like when Chatty McChatterson is *still talking* after you've tried ten different low-key interventions, and you finally have to look Chatty square in the eye with the kind of gaze that shoots straight out the back of

Chatty's head, and say in the firm way that your *I mean business* momma said to you as a child, "STOP. IT. NOW."

Who are you to sell? As a reminder, you're an education professional! That's absolutely all that matters. What do you know? You know your content, you know your kids, and you know what works (and doesn't) in your classroom. What about the fear that anybody could make what you're selling? Sure, *maybe* they could make it, but here's the key distinction: *they aren't.* If they were, they wouldn't be coming to shop online. Here are a few types of teachers who may come to your store:

- ◆ **Brand new teachers.** They look for help with ideas that work! It's important to remember that not all new teachers have a colleague teaching the same language they teach. And even if they do have a colleague teaching the same language, they may not have a good relationship (yet) or the colleague may be a curriculum hoarder—"I had to make my own materials, so you have to as well." Maybe the new teacher inherited *nothing* from the teacher before them, and they are overwhelmed figuring out where to start. Conversely, they may have inherited an avalanche of materials from the previous teacher, and they don't know what is *good*...so they throw it all out.
- ◆ **Lost teachers.** Maybe they're lost in general (it happens), or maybe they're with a grade level they've never taught and truly don't know how to approach the content for this grade level.
- ◆ **Teachers forced to teach a class they have no background in.** You might not work somewhere where this happens, but that doesn't mean it isn't common practice elsewhere. I regularly read online about language teachers forced to teach a language they don't speak. (It often happens with French and Spanish.) My first year teaching I had to teach an Exploring World Cultures class in which I had to teach German, Arabic, Swahili, and American Sign for seven weeks. *I don't speak any of them.*
- ◆ **Teachers teaching a class for the first time.** Maybe Señor has taught Spanish 1 and 2 for ten years, but he was just

informed that he will have to teach AP Spanish Language next year...and the district won't pay for him to take the AP training...and he never even *took* AP Spanish as a *student*, let alone taught it...and there is no one else at the school who has taught it before.

◆ **Overwhelmed teachers.** Think of the teacher who has 4+ preps, a second job, her own kids at home, and coaches after school. She might *want* to create materials, but she simply doesn't have the time and/or energy. Something has to give, and if she can find excellent resources online with a few strokes of the keyboard, she'll do it.

◆ **Creativity-challenged teachers.** Some teachers plain ol' aren't very creative, but that doesn't mean they don't want to teach a creative lesson someone else wrote for them to beautifully execute! It's important for all of us to know our strengths and weaknesses and to have strategies in place to compensate for the weaknesses.

◆ **Teachers who lack a skill that you have.** Take tech, for example. Many teachers can *use it* but might not be great at the *creation* aspect. Another example is your level of fluency. Not everyone has the same level of target language fluency, and many teachers for whom language skills aren't their strength (maybe they're better at making connections with kids, for example) are looking for resources made by more knowledgeable teachers in their target language.

◆ **Bored teachers.** Sometimes we all get in a rut and look to others for some fresh ideas. This tends to happen in cycles and will happen several times over the course of a career.

◆ **Veteran teachers.** Veteran teachers often get assigned brand new classes (because of their expertise). They know the value of a solid activity (that you're selling!), and they have the money to buy it. Veteran teachers also will periodically fall into the "bored" camp, and they will seek out new strategies, resources, and ideas to once again make their teaching fresh.

◆ **Non-teachers.** There are people out there teaching (in schools and at home) who are not trained teachers. Their students deserve high-quality curriculum and resources, but they might not be the best ones to create it.

Simply put: know yourself, know your potential pool of buyers, and understand that they are not one and the same. The broader your view of your buyers, the greater your sales and earning potential.

8

There Is Only One You

Finding Your Niche

With any luck, your brain is abuzz! You're thinking about the amazing curriculum you know how to create, and you're envisioning the paycheck coming in. As you should! The next step before you set up more in your store is defining your niche. This is what will make your store stand out among all the other sellers and earn you repeat customers.

Every seller should consider what he or she has to sell in two main categories: 1) My niche; 2) Absolutely everything else that I know how to create well (because *it's a numbers game!*). In my opinion, it's not an exaggeration to say that 99% of the most successful online curriculum stores follow this principle.

Think of it like an investment portfolio. You might have some of your retirement investments in your district-sponsored 403(b) plan, you have a pension from your state, you have a Roth IRA, your friend wants you to go in on a hot little piece of real estate for a rental property, and you've invested in Netflix's stock because you figure you're keeping the company afloat yourself. One of those is likely where you are putting the bulk of your energy (i.e., your niche), but it's smart to have the others because when they work together you have a better chance at more money! It's the same with your original resources store.

You might know right away what your niche is. Fantastic! But it's not uncommon to have no idea, so use this workspace to get you thinking:

☁ WORKSPACE

Defining Your Niche

Your niche could be...	Examples	What do you think? What do you have in this category?
A class you teach	◆ IB French ◆ Exploring German ◆ AP Spanish	
A specific kind of product	◆ SMART board activities ◆ Videos ◆ Classroom posters (vocab, geography, etc.)	
A skill/expertise (Note: these don't necessarily translate directly to products, but it can be the angle you use to promote your store)	◆ A doctorate ◆ Native speaker	
A passion or particular creative focus	◆ Original grammar and vocab songs ◆ History-based lessons ◆ Art-based lessons	
An activity	◆ Games ◆ Group projects ◆ Reading strategies	
A high-need and/or low-curriculum area	◆ Japanese ◆ Heritage speakers ◆ Arabic	
A geographic area and/or language variant	◆ North Africa ◆ Central American Spanish ◆ Canadian French ◆ Austrian German	

You might find it helpful here to talk to—or simply listen to—your colleagues. What do your colleagues tell you you're good at? What do they like to use that you created? What sort of materials do they ask you for? If there is an answer to those questions that comes up again and again, that's an indication that it might be your niche!

9

It's Starting to Get Real

Uploading Your Free Item

If you're store is on the TpT platform, to finish up your seller account and officially have a functioning store, you need to upload one, featured, free item. There are millions of free items available (both as the primary featured items and not), and this wealth of resources created by teachers, not companies, is an absolute treasure trove for buyers. Pure genius on the part of the site's founders, to be sure!

So what should you upload as your free item? Choose an item that fits the following four criteria:

♦ **Valuable.** Your featured free item is not the time to pick something that you would've uploaded for free anyway. It should be worth something. You want your buyers to feel like they're getting a great deal snagging this item for free! It's also not the time to pick something about an obscure topic, as your free item should be a hot commodity that a lot of teachers could, would, and *will* use. "If it's so valuable, why would I want to list it as my free item? I could make money off it!" you might wonder. Think of it this way: you won't make *any* money if you don't get people into your store. This free item is "taking one for the team," the "team" being your store. If your free item is enticing enough, buyers will appreciate it, follow your store, and keep coming back. A free item can and should make you money—just not in the way you might initially think.

◆ **Indicative of your skill.** Choose a free item that showcases your overall work, and absolutely make sure your language is on point. If your niche is something that a lot of other teachers could use, then it could be a good time to showcase your niche. Conversely, it's not wrong to choose something from your "everything else" body of work if a high percentage of teachers of your language could use it. Either way, you want to pick an item that shows what *you* do *well*. It could be a grammar explanation, a game, or a CI activity, for example. That's irrelevant. What *does* matter is that it's professional.

◆ **Clear.** I cannot stress this point enough: your free item absolutely must have a clear product description in your store *and* have clear directions within the item itself. Failure to do either is detrimental to success. We'll talk more in Section 2 about how to write clear product descriptions and directions, but for now, think about how you write substitute teacher lesson plans: make these descriptions idiot-proof. (I'm not calling subs idiots here! Subs who speak our target language are few and far between, so unless we want to come back to a mess, we need to make sure there is no room for error in our notes and directions. The same goes with your free item.)

◆ **Linkable.** You don't want your featured free item to be a one-off item that doesn't connect to anything else you will eventually have in your store. Your featured free item should be related to a collection of other items you'll later upload for a *price*. That way, once you've uploaded those other items (more on this in Section 2), you can go back to your free item and hyperlink it to the related items with a message like this: "If you found this product helpful, I'm so glad! If you're teaching a unit about X, your students might also benefit from *this item* or my *bundle* that gives you even more practical and fun resources at a discounted price!"

It's important to remember that the featured free item is just that: *featured*. It's the primary free item that a potential buyer will see when they visit your store, but that doesn't mean it has to be (or should be) the *only* free item. Your free items might be resources you originally priced so low that you now think, "Meh. I'll just make it free. $0.25 isn't necessary," or they may be items you made free from the start. For many sellers, regularly listing free items in their store is a way to keep customers happy and coming back.

10

Get Organized

Setting Your Preliminary Categories

In a major department store, you'll see a map that helps you navigate your way through the store: bedding, women's, men's, jewelry, shoes, and so on. When setting up your TpT store, you'll see *Custom Categories* and *Manage Your Categories* under that. That's what you'll use to set up your categories, which are simply different areas of your World Language "department" store.

There are some key *Dos* and *Don'ts* when choosing categories:

- **DO hunt around.** Take a look at other World Language stores for ideas. What patterns do you see? Don't be tricked into thinking your categories need to be different than those of other sellers either. There are common themes in categories for a reason: the items in those categories *sell*. Choose categories that showcase your niche(s) as well as the "everything else I can create" items.

- **DON'T name categories after classes.** What is German 1 material to you might be Exploring German or German 2 to someone else. If you're particularly drawn to labeling resources in that fashion, a better approach would be using language like *Beginning High School German*, *Intermediate High School German*, and *Advanced High School German*, as those allow for more flexibility.

- **DO make them specific, but DON'T go *too* specific.** That can be confusing, so here's an example: let's say you have some activities for numbers. Putting them in a category called *Basics* is too broad. That could encompass greetings, letters, numbers, some initial verbs, a few adjectives...who knows? What's "basic" to you might not be "basic" to someone else. Conversely, it's too specific to make a category called *Numbers 0–10*. If you break it down that far, you could have ten categories with numbers alone! It's all about finding the sweet spot.

◆ **DO be clear.** One or two words is generally best, and try to use the words that are most commonly used for the topic. For example, if you have a lot of activities about accent marks, call the category *Accents* or *Accent Marks*, not *Diacritical Marks*. Even though the latter may be more accurate, it's not the most used.

◆ **DO think beyond World Language topics.** A category named *Numbers* might be obvious to you because it's a common topic in the World Language classroom, but there are topics in the more general realm of *Education* that are useful as categories too. For example, 2020 saw the rise of the *Distance Learning* category. Conveniently, a product can also be tagged in more than one category, so that activity you created for the numbers 0–59 in German can easily be tagged in *Numbers, Telling Time,* and *Distance Learning.* A variety of World Language topics *and* general education topics is best.

Again, that pesky issue of language choice comes up for us. *Do I label my categories in English or in the Target Language?* As with store names, it's fine to do either, ultimately, but naming your categories in English (or at least making them bilingual) will reach a larger audience. Consider the teacher who has never taught Spanish in his life but his district was desperate and figured, "He already teaches French, so isn't there a lot of language learning crossover? Surely he can teach Spanish 1!" (We all know that this happens far more often than it should...which is never!) That teacher is more likely to search for resources using English key words.

Don't stress about categories. Whatever you choose when you are setting up your store will absolutely evolve over time. To get started, five to ten categories is perfect. As your store grows, you'll change the categories you started with to better reflect your offerings. Nothing in your store is a permanent choice.

💭 WORKSPACE

Choosing the Right Categories

_____

Upon first thought...
What are the categories that come to mind right away, based on what you like to create and what your skills are?

After some hunting...
Check out at least ten other World Language stores. Shoot for at least three of them being outside of your target language, just to provide variety. What do you see? What could work for you too? What do you see that you don't like and want to stay away from?

As you build your store, always remember:
Your buyers aren't all like you.

11

Legal Talk
Staying Lawsuit-Free

Many teachers work second (and third…and fourth…) jobs, and I am no exception. Moonlighting as an attorney, however, isn't one of them. (Bummer!) The information I share here is not to be mistaken for professional legal advice; however, legal issues are absolutely important to address. It is my intention to share important considerations and to encourage you to follow through and seek your own legal advice from a professional when it's appropriate for you.

Shift your lens:
Your store is a commercial enterprise, a business.

Let that sink in. You are no longer solely a teacher, sharing curriculum with colleagues; you're CEO of your store. Your job is not "just" to create high-quality content for *your* students. You now create for *all* students while you simultaneously focus on growth, sales, and earnings. You are an expert in your field, so you are a perfect candidate to create the highest quality curriculum out there and be compensated for it. I just recommend doing it legally.

Full disclosure: I'm about to share two statements that have no grounding in actual fact. I have not surveyed online curriculum sellers, nor have I asked a curriculum platform if it has collected this kind of data itself. It is entirely my opinion that the following is true:

1. 99% of sellers have not hired an Intellectual Property (IP) lawyer.
2. 99% of sellers infringe on IP law in their stores.

The likely reason for the first statement is that when teachers hear "lawyer" they go straight to "wildly expensive." While it's true that they *can* be costly, it's also true that in many towns and cities there are groups (e.g., Small Business Associations) that offer consults with various kinds of lawyers pro bono. It's worth looking into, if for no other reason than to sleep more soundly!

The reason I believe the second statement is that I don't think most sellers *know* they're infringing on IP law. It's not about trying to get out of something or being sneaky. It is simply a lack of information on the part of well-intentioned people.

Let's look at one area of teacher contracts. I am an American who teaches in a public school, so if that is not your situation, know that there is some digging you have to do to find out specifics of your contract. In most American public schools, including all of them that I have worked for, there is a piece of our contract that basically states:

If your product was created on The District's contract time

or

on a District device

or

for the express purpose of using it with students in The District...
it is the intellectual property of The District.

Now, I know, I know...this doesn't make sense at all. Not to teachers, anyway. We created the materials! A lot of it we created at home on the weekend! The district had nothing to do with what a success my awesome project on Central American Spanish-speaking countries is for kids! I agree 100%, but it's still in (most of) our contracts. Furthermore, it's actually common practice in most non-education fields. Because it's a pretty sweet deal for districts, it's not going away any time soon.

Some teachers would argue right away, "I don't want to use my personal time for school work!," but this is not your time as a teacher; this is your time as a CEO. Spending a couple hours here and there creating products to sell is no different than spending a couple hours at a waitressing job or driving for Lyft. The key difference, for me, is that the time I spend creating products to sell is professionally enhancing. (That, and I can do this job in my pajamas and with a glass of wine!)

That piece of American public school contracts doesn't encompass all of Intellectual Property (IP) law, however, so what's the answer, then? The most obvious solution for every seller is to hire an IP lawyer to make sure the products you're selling are on the up-and-up. If you can't afford a consultation with an IP lawyer at the start of your store, I recommend building that into your plan and looking for pro bono consults in the meantime.

Build the cost of an IP lawyer into your plan.

After a couple of years of having a TpT store, my initial revenue goal materialized. I decided to invest some of my store's earnings back into the store by hiring a knowledgeable IP lawyer, and I have returned to him with more questions since that initial consultation. Does it cost money? Yes. Am I more comfortable and confident in my business because of it? Absolutely. (A nice perk is that the cost of the lawyer is a tax write-off for me because it counts as a business expense. More on this in the tax chapter in Section 3.)

Some sellers also choose to make their store a Limited Liability Company (LLC). An LLC puts more distance between your personal finances/assets and those of the business (i.e., your TpT store). Creating an LLC is easily Google-able, and although it's different everywhere, it's relatively cheap and simple to do. Additionally, many towns' Small Business Associations offer free mentors. These professionals are a wealth of knowledge and can help walk you through the LLC process quite easily. (Although mentors are free, I recommend treating them to coffee or tea while they give you advice.)

The curriculum sales platforms have good resources about copyright and intellectual property, which I encourage you to check out. Chances are, your questions have been asked by other sellers too.

After all of this, you may think, "I bet I've seen products on TpT that aren't fully legal!" Yeah...*maybe*. But it's like I heard my dad tell me a million times growing up: *Worry about yourself; it's a full-time job*. We have no way of knowing if another seller has a legal permission that we don't, and there definitely are sellers whose lawyers have done the work to get those permissions. Every minute you spend worrying about another seller is time that could've been spent creating products, and you know what that means: you're missing out on money because *it's a numbers game*. It isn't worth it. Let it go.

Venturing into the legal realm can seem daunting, confusing, and even downright scary. Just remember that if you feel any of those things it's likely because, for most people, IP law is an area you know little to nothing about. Once you start learning and gaining knowledge of the subject, however, it will feel considerably more manageable. When seeking expertise, there's nothing wrong with starting small.

WORKSPACE

Here is a sample list of questions to ask professionals (some free, some paid) who can help your business grow.

Topic and Question to Ask	To Whom do I Direct the Question?	Answer
Work for Hire—Does my district allow me to sell work I created for use with my students in the district?	District office and/or union	
Intellectual Property Policy—Am I allowed to sell work I created on a school device? Is it different for during school hours vs. non-school hours?	District office and/or union	
FERPA law—What do I need to do with my products to comply with FERPA?	Union rep or union lawyer	
Creating an LLC—I'd like to be CEO of my business and my business's primary worker. How do I do that?	Lawyer, business coach, or Small Business Association mentor	
Trademark law—How do I avoid illegally using an image or words?	Lawyer	
Copyright law—How do I avoid infringing on copyrighted material?	Lawyer	
Commercial licenses—How do I obtain commercial licenses for fonts, images, etc.? Is it different from product to product?	Lawyer	
Derivative law—I would like to sell materials that align with a copyrighted resource (e.g., a textbook, a movie, a novel). How can I legally do that?	Lawyer	

Section 1 Homework

It's time to put these principles into action! Here is a checklist of items to complete:

- Create a seller account
  - ◊ Choose Basic or Premium.
  - ◊ Choose a store name and image.
  - ◊ Link a new email address to the account. Use your store's logo/image as the image attached to the email account as well.
  - ◊ Choose/Set up a payment method. (I didn't cover this in Section 1 because this is a piece of technology that can change over time. Choose whatever is the best option for you of the options available at the time.)
- Spend time researching other sellers
  - ◊ What do you like? What don't you like?
  - ◊ What gives you ideas/inspiration?
  - ◊ Are there common themes? That means those areas already have "proof of concept" (i.e., they work)
- Upload your featured (free) item
- Create at least five categories
  - ◊ You'll add more later, but five is a great start!
- Ask legal questions of professionals
  - ◊ Start with the ones that are free!

◆ Complete the workspace pages
  ◊ These are great to come back to over time. You might go on a run with an idea, and when you've seen that through, you can come back to your workspace pages and pick a new idea to run with.

Congratulations! You officially have a functioning store! In Section 2, we focus on filling your store effectively because—say it again for the cheap seats!—*it's a numbers game!*

SECTION 2
Filling Your Store

12

You Have More Than You Think

Creating Products

Now the most fun part can begin: filling your online store! I approach this section as though you already have a (large or small) stockpile of products that are ready to upload and sell, but if you don't yet, it's okay. You can absolutely create and upload products as you go because these concepts still stand.

Golden Rule for Selling Curriculum Online:
It's a numbers game.

The Golden Rule for Selling Curriculum Online will be your guide throughout this section. If you want to reach your sales goals, you absolutely cannot get around uploading product after product...*after product*. Not only are you CEO of your store, but you're also your own, private, curriculum-writing factory of one!

Arguably the biggest obstacle to sales is a mindset that limits what you created and, therefore, can upload and sell. The idea is to start with something you have, and then branch off in as many ways as you can. Let's look at some examples as if we were talking about your products together.

As I've said before, we are language professionals. That means that if we have only created the one product we *think* we have, it shouldn't take us very long to branch out and create more products.

TABLE 12.1

WHAT YOU THINK YOU HAVE	WHAT YOU ACTUALLY HAVE
"I have a handout to introduce reflexive verb formation in present-tense Spanish. That's just *one* product."	"No, you have at least *six* products." ◆ The handout you think you have (more word-based) ◆ Version B of the same handout (more image-based) ◆ A worksheet that can go with either version ◆ A reflexive verb quiz ◆ Version B of a reflexive verb quiz ◆ A bundle with all of these items
"I have a guide for a ten-chapter novel in German that is in the public domain. That's just *one* product."	"No, you have at least 23 products." ◆ A guide for each of the ten chapters ◆ A bundle with all of the chapter guides ◆ A quiz for each of the ten chapters ◆ A final project ◆ A bundle with all of the chapter guides, all of the quizzes, and the final project
"I have a true/false quiz for a francophone Africa unit. That's just *one* product."	"No, you have at least *seven* products." ◆ The quiz you think you have ◆ Version B of the same quiz ◆ A bundle with both quizzes ◆ A multiple-choice version of the quiz ◆ A short answer version of the quiz ◆ A PowerPoint with discussion questions that relate to the quiz ◆ A bundle with all the quizzes and the discussion questions

With some of the products above, you might wonder, "But why would anyone buy that?" Trust me: It will sell.

◆ **Quizzes.** Buyers often want to buy multiple versions of quizzes so that they can use one as a practice quiz and one as the graded quiz. Alternatively, some want more than one version so that they can give a different version to each class.

◆ **Bundles.** Earnings potential is huge with bundles. Make different bundles to anticipate buyer needs (e.g., High School, Middle School, and Elementary School bundles;

Present-Tense, Past-Tense, and Future-Tense bundles.)
There is more on bundles later in this section.

◆ **Individual chapters.** Never forget that your buyers
aren't you. Just because you are teaching a full novel
doesn't mean someone else is. Buyers might already have
resources for *part* of the novel, but not all of it, and they
might not do assessments with the same frequency as
you. Always create for more than one type of buyer.

◆ **Organizational tools.** Products like day-by-day directions for students that teachers can post on a screen in the
classroom (e.g., "Today in class we are... Tomorrow we
are...) help teachers establish class flow and help students
stay on track. Unit plans and semester plans that outline
what you do, when you do it, and for how long you do
it also sell well, particularly for first-year teachers or for
those teaching a class for the first time because teachers
in those situations are often unsure of pacing.

Additionally, you can effectively *double* the number of products
you create and sell by making multiple versions of the same item.
By that, I mean creating them with different technology. For
example, you could make and sell a Word version *and* a Google
Doc version of a resource. If you have access to Microsoft Office
(Word, Excel, PowerPoint, etc.) at school or at home, this probably
doesn't make sense to you. But remember: not all buyers have the
same situation as you. Some districts and schools don't pay for
Microsoft Office; instead, they rely exclusively on Google products. Now *some* Word and PowerPoint files will open beautifully
in Google Docs and Slides, respectively, but not all will open
properly. Even if the files do open properly, it's better customer
service to take the guess work out of it for the buyer and simply
sell the product in the format the buyer is looking for to begin
with.

💭 WORKSPACE

You Have More Than You Think

Write three products you created that you think comprise good, high-quality curriculum that could be useful to another teacher.	How might these products easily and quickly morph into more? What else could you make from those three products?

1. _____
   _____

   • _____
   • _____
   • _____
   • _____
   • _____
   • _____
   • _____

2. _____
   _____

   • _____
   • _____
   • _____
   • _____
   • _____
   • _____
   • _____

3. _____
   _____

   • _____
   • _____
   • _____
   • _____
   • _____
   • _____
   • _____

***You always have more products to create
than you think.***

13

If You Upload It, It Will Sell

Using Best Practices

Much like in *Field of Dreams* ("If you build it, they will come") or *Wayne's World 2* ("If you book them, they will come"), if you upload a quality product to TpT, it will sell!

It's okay to have a small amount of skepticism; I get it. Keep in mind, however, that TpT is a business, and you are the head of your store. Most teachers' level of knowledge in running an online store is significantly less than what they know about running a classroom. Always keep in mind that your buyers aren't you and that you don't know who is out there. In other words, what *buyers* purchase might not be what *you* would purchase, and because everyone is in a different situation, everyone has a different reason for what they buy.

One of the first products I ever uploaded was a rubric for grading speaking assessments. I went back and forth for quite a while about whether or not to even upload it because it seemed too "simple." It took me only about ten minutes to create, I was selling it for $0.50, and I kept thinking, "Ugh, *anyone* could make this. Why would anyone buy it?" Several years later, it remains one of my most frequently sold products, and I have increased the price! While it's true that buyers *could* make whatever it is that you're selling on their own, the fact remains that they *don't*.

When considering your current and future products, keep these three Best Practices in mind:

♦ **Products should be editable.** When sellers first open a store, there is a tendency to create and sell non-editable products, exclusively. The fear is that if someone has an editable game, for example, they'll use it as a template to create more games on their own for any topic of their choice instead of buying more from that seller. On the surface, that feels like a reasonable concern. But here's a secret about buyers: 99% of them will not do this. They don't have any desire to recreate your product. Like, *zero*. They're busy people, and they want to buy. By making your products editable, it allows buyers to change one or two little pieces to fit their classroom and their students. This is related to the "offense style" of customer service we'll talk about later.

♦ **Products should include answer keys.** While the fear about making products editable relates more to teachers, the fear about including an answer key relates more to students. Some teachers worry that if students know about the online curriculum store they may buy products just to get the answer keys to use to cheat. First of all, this would primarily apply only to high school students because they're the ones with jobs and money. However, the idea of high school students taking time out of their jam-packed social and extracurricular schedules to find out where their teacher buys curriculum, hunt down the specific product, and buy it in time to cheat with it is about as likely as Tom Hanks making a bad movie. It's probably not going to happen! It's best to provide proactive customer service to the teacher and include the answer keys right from the start. When buyers know that a particular store's products always include answer keys, which then saves them time and effort, they will buy again!

♦ **Products should be CLEAR...but they also should be CREATIVE and/or PRACTICAL.** Absolutely every single product you upload needs to be CLEAR if you hope to sell it. There is no way around this. Each product needs to include instructions, baby step by baby step, for both the teacher and the students, so there is no room for error. Approach directions for students and the teacher like you would approach writing a sub plan. To illustrate this point, consider a seller I know who used to include language BINGO boards in product bundles. This seller didn't include instructions because it seemed unnecessary…it's *BINGO*! Then came a bad review from a buyer specifically because she didn't include directions for, you guessed it, BINGO! (Note: online curriculum platforms are international, so it's possible this buyer was someone whose culture doesn't include BINGO as a game everyone knows.) Once you have determined a product is CLEAR, there's one more step: each product needs to be CREATIVE and/or PRACTICAL. Countless teachers don't feel naturally creative, and they are specifically looking for products that stretch beyond what they are capable of making. Conversely, other teachers are all about products that are practical and that provide solid value because of their uses and applications.

As with any business, it's essential to do some market research with these principles. What do your buyers need? What are they looking for? What do they want but struggle to create themselves? These questions can be answered with a little effort by visiting teacher blogs, attending World Language teacher conferences, or reading the market research trends in the Seller Update TpT emails, but it also can be much simpler. If you tune into what your colleagues are saying in department meetings, a wealth of information is shared. Use this information to direct what your next product line will be!

Ultimately, it all boils down to a handy little rhyme:

> *Is it good for students and written well?*
> *Upload it now! It will sell!*

14

Customer Service Strategy #1

Playing Offense

The way I see it, customer service is 50% preventative, 48% engaging with customers, and 2% dealing with unhappy customers and negative reviews. The 50% that is preventative is what I like to refer to as Offensive Customer Service. It's our game plan that we're bringing to the court, regardless of what the other team (i.e., the buyer) does. It's the work we put into our products before they're even officially uploaded onto our platform. In short, it's writing quality product descriptions, writing clear directions, and offering ideas on variations.

Take time now to do Step 1 of the workspace at the end of the chapter. This is to help you get a read on where you're at with product descriptions. After learning more, you'll come back to Step 2.

Hands-down, the #1 method to prevent negative reviews and, therefore, have a strong offensive strategy, is to write high-quality product descriptions. As a seller, it is your job to write a detailed and honest description each and every time. Too often, sellers mistakenly think brevity is best, but that is a recipe for a bad review.

TABLE 14.1

PRODUCT DESCRIPTION	NEGATIVE REVIEWS THAT WILL COME IN
This is a Jeopardy-style game to review –AR verbs. *(Seems clear enough, right? Wrong!)*	♦ Ugh! This is all in SPANISH! I can't use it! ♦ It's okay, but it doesn't work with Google Slides. Disappointing. ♦ There are no directions! How do you play? I couldn't use this. ♦ This had some weird formatting issues that I had to fix. ♦ I'm asking for a refund. This is a PowerPoint file, and my district doesn't have access to Microsoft Office programs. ♦ All of these verbs are in the present tense. I wish there were more variety. ♦ Why aren't there any irregular –AR verbs? These are all regular and, quite frankly, just too simple for my students.

Yikes, right? Although some of the negative comments above may seem irrational, they are absolutely all variations of negative reviews I have seen or heard of personally. So what, then, should your product descriptions include? What can you do to be clearer and avoid negative reviews? You'll never completely get rid of negative reviews or unhappy customers, but there are a few items to include in your descriptions that will help you have a strong offensive strategy:

1. **What the item *is*.**
2. **What the item is *not*.**
3. **Why you chose one option over another.**
4. **A list of what is on each page of the product.**
5. **Why you like the product or why it works well with students.**
6. The duration of the activity, **game, etc., takes in class.**
7. **Hyperlinks to other products in your store.**

Here is what that would look like using the product from Table 14.1

TABLE 14.2

NEW PRODUCT DESCRIPTION

This is a Jeopardy-style game to review regular present tense –AR verbs in Spanish. It is a PowerPoint document, not Google Slides, and it was created on a Mac. (If you use it on a PC, there may be very slight formatting changes you'll want to make.)

This product would be great for Level 1 Spanish students who are just learning regular –AR verbs in the present tense, but it also would be useful as a review at the start of Level 2. Because it is geared toward early-level Spanish learners, many of the questions are in English and require responses from students in Spanish. There are some questions that are in Spanish, but they are appropriate for early-level Spanish students.

This product includes <u>vosotros</u> examples, but they are editable if you want to swap them out. I include them to create a more global view of the language.

I love that it's a team game, and in the second slide of the game file I outline two different ways of playing (in English). I recommend letting each class choose how they want to play! This game typically lasts up to 45 minutes, depending on your students and class pace.

This download includes:

1. The Jeopardy-style game in a PowerPoint file.
2. A Word document with instructions for the teacher.

If you are teaching regular –AR verbs in Spanish, you may be interested in my bundle of regular –AR verb activities, sold at a discounted price <u>here</u>.

Not all buyers will want to read the full product description—some will know what a Jeopardy-style game is, have all the tech tools they need, run with it, and love your product! Others, however, will read your full description and will ultimately find out if the product *is* or is *not* right for them and their classroom. You never know who the buyer will be, so writing a description that will reach buyers' potential questions is key.

Closely related to the product description is the product title. For World Language teachers, this brings up the continual issue of language choice. Because the majority of the users on curriculum selling platforms are native English speakers, I recommend putting the bulk of your product titles in English. Writing titles in English works well, and including some of the target language via repetition (e.g., Family Vocabulary/*la Famille*) is fine as well, but it is my opinion that titles completely in the target language limit your audience for most products. Additionally, foreign characters in titles can be problematic, depending on the device used.

Now it's time to circle back to the workspace at the end of the chapter. In Step 2, rewrite your product description based on what you have now learned.

I firmly believe that the product description is the most important piece of "offense-based" customer service because it can ward off issues even before the product is purchased. After the product is purchased, however, two other aspects of a seller's arsenal become key players as well: clear directions and ideas for variations.

Buyers—and teachers, in general—don't want to mess around. They want to buy a resource that makes their lives easier, not harder. Therefore, it is the seller's job to do everything to make sure that happens. The directions given in a resource are there for that purpose. The directions should cover two areas: what the *students* should do, and what the *teacher* should do.

- ◆ **Student directions.** The directions for the students will be in the product itself. They can be in English or the target language (this often depends on the level of the student,) but clarity is key. You can even put the directions in *both* languages and write in the directions for the teacher that they should choose what set of directions they want to use and delete the other set. For small activities, be brief, and always give an example for students to follow. For larger activities or projects, it is often helpful to list directions in a step-by-step format.
- ◆ **Teacher directions.** The directions for the teacher will be in a separate page. Here, it's perfectly acceptable to use only English. There are four main areas to cover: 1) What the teacher should do to prepare for the activity (e.g., copies, classroom setup); 2) How to group the students (if applicable); 3) Timing expectations (list what the teacher should do to guide the students through the activity, including the amount of time each step should take); and

4) Tips to keep the activity rolling smoothly. To be clear, I don't include separate teacher directions for *all* activities; for some of the larger and/or more complicated resources, however, it's a necessary addition that buyers appreciate.

There are many ways a learning resource can be interpreted. Because of that, and in an effort to support teachers who use your resources, it's never a bad idea to include a (short) list of variations to your activity. These variations can be seen as "extras" that enhance the value of the product for the buyer. For example:

- ◆ If you have mini white boards, you can… but if you don't, you can…
- ◆ If your class is large, try… but if your class is small, it will work better to…
- ◆ If you are teaching in a classroom, try… but if you're teaching remotely, try…
- ◆ One way of awarding points in this game is… but another is… Ask the students which way they would like to play!
- ◆ If students have 1:1 digital devices, it might work well to… but otherwise, you can…
- ◆ This is a simple worksheet that can be assigned as homework, but you can also turn it into a game by…

The resources you create will ultimately determine the best offensive game plan. It's wise to focus on the product description because every product you upload will need one. But depending on your resource, separate directions for the teacher and/or a list of possible variations on your product could benefit you (with a positive review) as well as your buyers.

💭 WORKSPACE

Product Descriptions

Step 1: Now
Think of any product you have, and write a description for it in the space below. This should be what you would type into the description field when uploading your product onto TpT.

Step 2: Later
I'll tell you when to come back to this part and what to do. For now, keep reading!

15

Sales Strategy #1

Bundling Your Products

What is a bundle? A bundle is a group of single items, packaged and sold together at a discount from the individual items' prices. Bundles are arguably your best opportunity to boost sales and, therefore, your earnings, because bundles typically have higher price points than most individual items.

TpT's structure has changed over the years, and bundles are one area in which TpT has made significant improvements. (This is precisely why this isn't a "click here...and then click this... and then go here..." book because tech changes too fast and too often!) The same may be true for other platforms.

It used to be that sellers had to create zip files of items they wanted to sell in a bundle and then upload the zip file as a single product. Buyers will still find many such zip file bundles, but the more recent trend is to allow sellers to bundle items in their stores with the click of a button. When you add a new product, you will see four options: Digital Download, Video, Online Resource, Bundle of Resources.

By selecting "Bundle of Resources," you can manually select which products in your store you want to include in the bundle as well as what percent discount or dollar amount discount you choose for the price. This is especially useful because when you update a single item (e.g., fix a typo, change clip art), it automatically will update in the bundle. Previously, sellers had to update the item in *each and every* zip file bundle that file was in!

No matter what platform you use, here are two recommendations for creating bundles:

♦ **Include clear descriptions.** We already covered writing complete product descriptions, but with a bundle it gets trickier because you don't want to write several paragraphs for each product in a 15-item bundle, for example. In this case, I recommend including a list of items in the bundle (the buyers can easily scroll down and see the items, but not all will do that), and include verbiage at the end along these lines: "For complete descriptions of products in this bundle, please see below and read details for each product included. If you have questions, please post them in the Q&A, and I will respond to them as soon as possible."

♦ **Don't do too deep of a discount.** Discounted bundles are great, but if you price your bundle at too deep a discount you risk losing more money than you maybe want to during sales. (More on sales in Section 3.) If a bundle is already 20% off the prices of individual items, and then a sale comes around during which you discount your whole store another 20%, the items in that bundle are now 40% off. That's great for buyers, but a discount that deep might not be where you want to go, earnings-wise. (Or maybe it is. Your call!)

After you create a few bundles, there's one more logical step: MEGA BUNDLES! For example, let's say you create five different resources for one past tense, and then you sell them as a bundle. Later, you create five different resources for a *different* past tense, and you bundle *those*. The next step is to create one, giant "mega bundle" that includes everything from both! Here's another example: If you're working with an IP lawyer, he or she could obtain permission from a textbook company for you to create resources expressly for their products. Once you have permission, you could create a bundle of resources for each unit in their

Level 1 book. Follow that by bundling all of *those* together into one mega bundle that includes all of the materials you made for all of the units in the Level 1 textbook. Then you can repeat the process for the Level 2 and Level 3 textbooks as well. Mega bundles are particularly fun because they have a higher price tag, so they earn you a higher commission!

16

Sales Strategy #2

Hyperlinking Your Products

Hyperlinking your products to each other is an effective way to showcase your store to potential buyers and hopefully secure repeat customers. Fortunately, hyperlinking is one of the simplest and fastest strategies to boost sales.

- ♦ **WHERE:** hyperlinking happens in your product description.
- ♦ **WHEN:** every product should hyperlink to at least one other product. Ideally, each item would hyperlink to a bundle.
- ♦ **HOW:** have you ever hyperlinked in an email, for example? It's the same. In your product description, highlight what you want to hyperlink, and then click the hyperlink icon. In the pop-up that follows, you'll copy and paste the URL to your other product or bundle.
- ♦ **WHAT TO WRITE:** sometimes you might hyperlink an item in a sentence within your description: "This matching quiz on Latin prefixes pairs perfectly with this quiz on Latin suffixes." More often, however, you will link your product to related items at the bottom of your description. Here's an example: "If you are teaching a unit on numbers, check out my Numbers Bundle, which includes

this product and a variety of related products sold at a discount." (Tip: don't mention the precise percentage discount of the bundle. It is very common for sellers to discount bundles at different rates and/or to change the discount after sales and ratings have gone up.)

Now is a good time to check back in on your featured free item. At a minimum, it should link to one other product in your store. It's even better if it links to a bundle!

17

Sales Strategy #3

Creating Templates

Creating templates from your products is an excellent way to boost sales. Because it is all about numbers, templates are an easy and fast way to take products you have already created, make them more general, and quickly expand both your store and your potential audience.

So what do I mean when I talk about making a template? Templates primarily fall into one of two categories:

- **Specific target language (TL) topic to general TL topic.** With this approach, you take a specific product that you made, and you break it down to make it more general, yet it still remains a product for other teachers of your TL See Table 17.1.
- **Specific TL topic to general topic for** *any* **TL.** Here, you start with a product that you made, and you make it much more general, in English, and useable for nearly any World Language teacher. This opens up your potential buyer audience because you won't only select *your* TL, but other TLs as well, when you fill out the "Add New Product" page on TpT and select a Subject Area. I recommend selecting your TL, World Language (in general), and Spanish, if you're not already uploading a Spanish product, because this is likely the largest group of WL buyers. See Table 17.2.

TABLE 17.1

PRODUCT YOU HAVE	TEMPLATE IT COULD BECOME
Italian: A conjugation game for –ARE verbs.	A blank game that could be used for any regular verb group: –ARE, –ERE, or –IRE. Must include directions for the teacher to plug in useful verbs for what his/her class is studying.
German: A cartoon strip product with images from *Hansel and Gretel*. Students have to write conversation for each illustration.	A blank cartoon strip product for any Grimm fairy tale with directions in German. Students have to do the illustrations and write conversation for key events in the story.
Arabic: A web quest activity for Egypt.	A generalized web quest handout that would work for any Arabic-speaking country.

TABLE 17.2

PRODUCT YOU HAVE	GENERAL TEMPLATE IT COULD BECOME
Japanese: A rubric for a writing assessment after a unit on *Kazoku* (family).	A rubric for a writing exam in any language. The rubric must be in English.
Chinese: A mini-project on Chinese New Year foods.	A project guide for holiday foods from any country. This project guide must be in English.
Arabic: A guide for critiquing a new Arabic-language video and song from Lebanese singer Elissa.	A guide for critiquing a new video and song from any country and artist or group. This guide must be in English.

Templates are an easy way to boost sales and the total number of items in your store. Often, when you make a template of a resource that works well, you can keep coming back to that template again and again, topic after topic. They also benefit sellers with *time* because once you have a template complete, making multiple versions of that resource to fit different topics goes much faster than the creation of the initial template.

💭 WORKSPACE

Creating Templates

Write down three products you created that you are excited about.	What kind of template could these products become? These could either be for other teachers of your TL or for any WL teacher.
1. ------------------------------------	• ------------------------------------
2. ------------------------------------	• ------------------------------------
3. ------------------------------------	• ------------------------------------

Two kinds of templates:

1. General template for your target language
2. General template for any target language

18

Sales Strategy #4

Establishing Curb Appeal

Anyone who has ever bought or sold a home is undoubtedly familiar with the term "curb appeal." The premise is that the inside of the house may be amazing, but if you can't get people in the door because of the way the outside of the house and/or the yard looks, it doesn't matter. The same goes for your online store.

Part of curb appeal in the online curriculum resource world is your store name and logo, which we covered in Section 1. The other half of curb appeal, however, is your products themselves. It doesn't take long to hunt around on the site and see that there is a vast range of "looks" in the product covers and thumbnails. Many of them look, for lack of a better word, "cute," or like what a bulletin board in an elementary classroom might look like. Sellers will often buy specialty fonts, clip art, and programs to create this style.

It's common for new sellers to worry about this. *Do my products need to look like* that *to sell? Without that, can I even compete?* While I understand the desire to (attempt to) keep up with that trend, I don't think it's necessary. Here are a few points to consider.

There are certainly ways you can create "curb appeal" that don't cost a lot of (or any) money. A nice compromise is not focusing on creating a cute product but creating a well-designed *cover image*. That's not to say that a sloppy product will sell well or that it will earn you good reviews. It won't. You absolutely must have

TABLE 18.1

MAKING "CUTE" PRODUCTS

Pros	Cons
◆ This style can be especially appropriate for elementary students and classrooms. ◆ A fun look for your product covers may attract more people to your store, which, therefore, may lead to more sales. ◆ A fun look may give the impression of a more professional business, which may lead to more sales. ◆ You can easily find a lot of information about how to make your products look cute with a simple Google search because there are sellers who blog about it.	◆ Many sellers use this style on their product covers (i.e., the first page of the product document). This page isn't usually used by the buyer, but often gets printed, which is a waste of paper. ◆ Fun fonts might not translate to the computer your buyer is using. If they don't, this can potentially throw off formatting. ◆ If you want your fun font to show up on the buyer's computer, you can use uneditable document formats, such as PDFs, but we've already discussed the downfalls of that approach. ◆ Most of the fancy fonts, clip art, and programs used to create these products and product covers are *not* free. ◆ Some fancy fonts only use capital letters. If you use one of these fonts, you may not realize that you used different capitalization in different areas, simply by habit, because it doesn't show up. But when the buyer downloads the product, it'll show up in the font his/her computer translates it to and be disjointed.

a professional-looking product, but professional can mean simple, neat, and clean.

The cover image is the buyer's first glance at your product. An easy way to make the image colorful and eye-catching, yet simple and free, is to use PowerPoint or Google Slides. Simply make a slide with the product name (and any other information you like), and take a screen shot of it. When you upload your product, you'll upload your own thumbnails with that screenshot as your Main Cover. The other thumbnails can and *should* be images of your product so that the buyer can get a sense of what it is they're buying before they buy it, but this style of cover can be effective in its simplicity. (Note: Some sellers on TpT use Preview files and some don't. If your thumbnails include images of your product, then a Preview is often not a deal-breaker for most buyers.) While a Main Cover is required, extra thumbnails are optional.

As you create products and wonder whether or not it is worth your time, effort, and (potentially) money to use the design tools that create all of the "cute" products, I want to remind you of two things:

1. If you *want* to create that kind of look for your products, go for it! More power to you! But don't feel like you *have* to. It takes time and energy to do it, and many of the sellers who use that approach are not also teaching full-time. If it's too much time and stress, don't do it; if it seems like a fun challenge, tackle it!
2. There has never been a buyer who has ever said, "Gee, this resource is clear, practical, accurate, and my students loved it…but man, I wish I hadn't bought it because it doesn't have fun fonts and special clip art."

In short, don't let the time, energy, and resources that *other* sellers have determine how you run your store. Every seller is different, with different needs, different availability, and different resources. You do you.

19

Equity Matters

Integrating Social Justice into Our Work

Issues of equity and social justice should be at the forefront of every effective educator's mind. Students don't all have the same background, nor do they have the same needs, and those backgrounds and needs don't automatically sync with our own simply because we share a classroom. Our job is to educate *all* of our students, not just those whose background and place in this world we understand or identify with.

Before I continue, I need to be clear about what I mean by *equity*. Often, equity and equality are confused. For purposes of this book, *equality* refers to every student receiving the same thing (instruction, materials, resources, etc.) while *equity* refers to every student receiving what he or she needs to be successful. Another way to look at it is that equality keeps everything even so there is no movement, whereas equity levels the playing field, bringing all students to the same starting line at the same time.

Social justice, on the other hand, refers to the equitable distribution of wealth, opportunities, and privileges. Although various organizations outline different principles for social justice, common themes are the principles of equity, access, participation, and rights.

So, what does this have to do with our classroom? What does it have to do with our curriculum sales business? It means that we need to consider these issues when writing and selling curriculum. Just as not all buyers are like us, not all students are like us, nor are all students like our own students. Remember: we create resources at school *for our own students*; we create resources at home *for students whose teachers patronize our business*. Quite literally, the resources we post in our online stores can be used by students across the globe. (Pretty cool, huh?)

In a related vein, the resources we create aren't *solely* going to students either; adults (teachers) are buying these resources. Because of that, we must consider equity in both our resources themselves and in our instructions and extra information we give to the teacher.

There are a multitude of ways to make our resources and the curriculum we teach more equitable and socially just. Furthermore, as teachers become more and more educated on these issues, the list grows even further, and the ideas that were previously there morph and change. I offer up the following list not as a be-all and end-all, but rather, as a place to start the conversation about how we can make better, more equitable curriculum. Simple areas to start include:

◆ **Use global names.** Teachers often create resources using first names (e.g., Johnny, Suzy, Mr. Smith,) so this is an easy change. It is logical for World Language teachers to go right to, "No problem! How about I use names common to my target language?" and although that's a start, it doesn't automatically solve the issue. For example, as a French teacher, I could use Monique, Jean-Claude, Sophie, and Philippe in my examples...but where do Monique, Jean-Claude, Sophie, and likely Philippe live? Who are typically given those names? Because French is spoken on five continents, it's authentic and practical to stretch beyond borders and include other names that are popular in the greater Francophone world such as Farah (f.), Khalil (m.), Samia (f.), or Basem (m.) Directly related to names are pronouns. Does your target language have gender-neutral pronouns? If so, what are they? You may choose to teach these and to use them in your resources.

(Note: In the francophone world, there is a gender-neutral pronoun—*iel*(*s*)—but it is not found in every francophone country as of 2020. Your target language may have a similar situation.)

◆ **Use global images.** Just as it's important to use names that span the global reach of the languages we teach, it's also important to vary the images we use in our resources. There are many ways to obtain free or low-cost (legal) images to use in the resources that we sell, and Google is adept at telling us where we can find them. I encourage you to look for images that are representative of multiple countries that speak your target language, of course, but we can—and should—go further. Within the images that represent various countries, we should also vary the (apparent) socioeconomic status, ethnicity, and gender of the people in the photos.

◆ **Show a variety of families.** Families come in all different varieties. They always have, of course, but we're talking about it—and accepting it—now more than ever. It is common to cover the topic of families in our World Language curriculum, so, from the start, we should make the topic inclusive. Across the globe, there are single-parent families, two-parent families, and blended families. There are children who are raised by grandparents or other family members and children who are raised by a community of multiple families. Some kids are raised by parents of the same gender. There are poor families, rich families, and everything in between. The families of some children include only one race, and there are children whose families include a rainbow of skin colors. Consider all of these realities (and more!) when discussing and showing families and, of course, when creating resources about families to sell in your store.

◆ **Include different abilities.** Being able-bodied is often taken for granted, and including images and references to different abilities in our resources is important. This tends to be a little bit harder with images, but that does open up an appropriate place for discussion. For example, anyone who travels outside of the United States can easily see how accessible American schools, parks, and businesses are for citizens who are handicapped as compared to many countries. This topic would make an excellent area of exploration for students, and if you have a particular passion here, why not make resources to support it?

◆ **Educate yourself.** The year 2020 saw a significant and much-needed rally for social justice causes. At one point that year, all ten of the books on the *New York Times* best seller list had ties to social justice themes. Suddenly, there was widespread availability *and advertising* of free and paid trainings on a variety of social justice-related subjects. Many of them are tailored specifically to educators! Simply *telling* our students about what it takes to be educated isn't enough; we have to *model it* by continuing to grow our own knowledge base as well. Taking part in professional development on equity issues will help our practice as educators, but we can also use the knowledge to create more equitable and informed resources in our stores. (In section 3 we cover the topic of taxes, and depending on current laws, money you spend on professional development may be tax deductible.)

◆ **Check your own language.** When we educate ourselves on equity issues in education, a common outcome is a heightened awareness of our own language: what we say, how we say it, and to whom we speak. First, as a French teacher, it's common for us to start sentences in class with "French people...," when we talk about cultural or linguistic issues. But is this accurate? Sometimes. But other times we say this, we don't actually mean *French people*; we mean *French speakers*. There's a difference. The latter is significantly more inclusive, as it refers to both native speakers (e.g., French, Senegalese, Canadian, North African, Haitian) and non-native speakers. Second, you may also discover that you sometimes start sentences with, "In Spanish *they* say..." No, not "they." In your classroom you are all Spanish (or Chinese, or German, etc.) speakers now, for one, but we also don't want to "other" the cultures and people about which we're teaching our students. A better option is to use, "In Spanish *we* say..." Simple language changes in our classrooms and in the resources we create can help students feel connections to the cultures we're teaching.

♦ **Recognize school inequality.** I teach in the United States, and from what I've seen in my travels, most countries are like mine in that there is a wide range of funding for schools. Some schools have resources available to them that are new and on the cutting edge of education. Others, however, have decades-old textbooks (if they have them at all) and not enough desks for every student. And that's not even including the vast differences in technology available in schools! When we create resources as sellers, we would do well to consider the digital divide. If we create an awesome activity that relies on a SMART board, for example, is there a way we could modify it so that classrooms that don't have a SMART board could do a variation of the same activity? This way, students in underfunded schools can still have access to the same excellent and effective resources their counterparts in more privileged schools have, and we, as sellers, are able to expand our offerings quite easily! Additionally, if you create two different versions of the same activity, hyperlink them to each other in the product description. This helps direct buyers to the variation that will work best for their classroom.

♦ **Recognize various abilities.** Remember when we discussed offense-based customer service strategies? One way you could take that a step further is to include variations for the resources you create based on ability. For example, you could include alternate ideas for modifying the resource for different disabilities. Additionally, you could leave notes for the teacher (or even put them in your product descriptions) about pieces of the resource that were expressly included in order to hit common Individualized Education Program (IEP) or 504 Plan accommodations.

◆ **Highlight more than one country.** Highlighting more than one country is related to the point about checking our language. If I'm setting up the directions for a speaking activity, for example, I might create a scenario such as "Imagine it's your first day of school as an exchange student in France..." for students to talk about. There's nothing wrong with this...that is, if I vary my language. Do I use France in most of my examples? If so, it's time to add in Morocco, Tahiti, Cameroon, Haiti, or any number of other francophone countries. We should create resources that include a variety of countries and cultures, wherever possible. When we do that, we are more likely to be inclusive of multiple races, religions, socioeconomic status, customs, and schools of thought.

As I said before, the list above is not exhaustive, but it's a place to start. Why, again, are these points vital? Students need to see themselves in the curriculum. When they do, it opens up possibilities for more learning, better learning, and continued interest. In order for students to see themselves in the curriculum, they need resources that are inclusive and equitable. As curriculum writers and sellers, it is our job to write for *all* students. This practice is professional and equity-minded, and it makes the offerings in our store more valuable.

20

It's a Big World Out There

Capitalizing on Culture

In my opinion, capitalizing on culture is a huge market opportunity for online curriculum stores. First, in my experience, there is comparatively little curriculum out there that focuses on culture and does it in an effective and practical way for students. Second, if we create materials that focus on culture, those materials can often be used by teachers who are teaching units that may have much of their unit protected by intellectual property law. Culture, as a concept, is generally far more open. (Of course, a quick consult with a legal professional is never a bad idea. Remember: there are often opportunities to ask questions like this free of charge!)

When considering culture, here are some ideas for how you can use it to create resources:

♦ **Create resources for multiple countries.** Let's say you are a German teacher who has created a WebQuest activity about *German* culture. Make the same activity for each of the other five German-speaking countries. Now you have six resources to sell instead of one, and it all stemmed from creating one great template. (Then if you bundle all of them together you would have seven resources!)

◆ **Create resources for different accents/regional differences.** It can be interesting and fun for students to learn about the variety of accents and vocabulary from country to country in your target language. Accents, in particular, can be giggle-inducing for kids, particularly when activities require them to try their own hand at less familiar accents with more difficult sounds. This also provides a perfect opportunity to teach that there is no "right" linguistic variation, just as North American English is not superior British English or vice versa.

◆ **Create resources for different vocabulary/slang.** Youth culture is often an area of culture that's easily forgotten, but that doesn't mean it isn't (arguably) the most interesting aspect of culture to our students. Students love to learn new slang words and "texting lingo." A fun activity is translating *standard l*anguage to *texting* language and vice versa. It's easy to make a game or class competition out of that too! The only problem here is that, as with English, slang and texting language changes rapidly, so it's imperative to stay up to date and take resources out of your store as they become outdated.

◆ **Create resources for the arts.** The arts generally encompass areas of "big C" culture such as literature, visual art, theater/film, and music. As long as we stay within legal boundaries and respect intellectual property rights, creating cultural activities for the arts is often a big hit with students. This is also an excellent and easy place to pay attention to equity in our resources. Make sure you represent artists (in any subcategory of the arts) who are varied: women and men, black and white, young and old.

◆ **Create resources for the four modalities.** Reading, writing, listening, and speaking are four areas (modalities) that have long been at the forefront of language instruction. Let's say you create a reading activity for your lower-level Arabic class about Egyptian culture. A perfect way to expand that resource is to create similar resources for each of the other three modalities. After that, a next step might be rewriting the *exact same four activities* but tweaking the language to make it appropriate for a higher level of Arabic. That way, what started as just one activity has morphed into *eight*…and that's not even including any bundles you might make from these items!

◆ **Profit (literally!) from travel.** As World Language teachers, we hopefully all love to travel and to experience new cultures, people, places, customs, and languages. After all, isn't that a major reason for why we do what we do? To instill a love and global curiosity in our students? When we travel, we have opportunities to immerse ourselves in our target language and bring back what we learned and experienced. We can then create resources for other teachers and students with that information! Photos and videos are an excellent place to start. Sure, Google has a wealth of photos available on a million different topics, but do you have permission to use those in your resources? An appropriate solution is to take your own photos. Similarly, YouTube has videos on nearly everything we can imagine, but do you have permission to create resources for them? Again, why not record your own videos? If we make our own videos, which can be done at the click of a button on a smartphone, we have control over exactly what language is used and what images are shown. An extension of this idea is to interview people we know in other countries and use either the video or sound file to create resources. (Of course, it's always a good idea to ask for permission to use the interviews in products that you're selling!) We can easily create short interviews with native speakers about a variety of topics, and we can use those files to create multiple activities/resources to use the classroom.

Culture is a wonderful topic to expand on in your store because *all* buyers can use materials on culture. It doesn't matter what textbook they use (if any,) nor does it matter what readers, novels, or ancillary materials they use. It also doesn't matter if they teach on a block schedule, a traditional schedule, or a home school schedule. Culture is truly one major area that has no boundaries for sales.

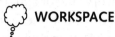 **WORKSPACE**

Culture and Me

Answer the following questions. Refer back to this workspace when you need inspiration about what resources you could create and sell next.

Where have I lived abroad, either studying or permanently?
What do I know best about that(these) place(s)?

Where do I often travel? What do I know best about that(those) place(s)?

Where do I have international friends? Would they be willing to do an interview with me? What could they talk about?

What do I have a lot of photos and/or video of?

Where am I going next? When? What could I record (photo, video) there that would be useful to other teachers?

What am I interested in linguistically?

What do I know a lot about in regard to the arts in my target language?

21

Show Me the Money

Pricing Products Fairly

One of the most common stressors for new curriculum sellers is the question of how to price products fairly. The TpT website has a FAQ page for sellers, which includes "How much should I charge for my products?" You may find it helpful to check that out and read the associated links. There are absolutely different schools of thought on product pricing, but one constant remains true: you can change prices any time!

Some sellers *start* pricing at $3.00. That may seem high, but the reason is purely strategic. With a Premium Seller account on TpT, the only time a transaction fee is involved is when a buyer's purchase is less than $3.00. Specifically, the fee is $0.15 per resource if the purchase total is less than $3.00. If no product in your store is less than $3.00, you avoid that fee altogether. (Reminder: Basic Seller accounts are charged a $0.30 per resource transaction fee.)

If that isn't the direction you want to take, I recommend starting by hunting around (again) on other World Language store sites and looking for pricing patterns. What do you notice? Are there pricing trends for various kinds of items? After you gather that research, here are follow-up questions to ask when pricing your product:

♦   Is this resource flexible? Can it be used multiple times and be modified to fit the buyer's classroom and students?

◆ How big is the product? (For example, a one-page handout should be priced lower than a ten-page project guide.)

◆ Does this resource fill a niche? Would it be hard for other
teachers to create?

◆ Is this resource in low or high demand?

◆ Is this resource in low or high supply? Are other sellers
selling similar products?

◆ How much work was involved in creating this product?

◆ What would I (fairly) pay for this product? A general rule
of thumb is $1.50 per page of content.

During your research, you may have noticed that the actual *numbers* used in the prices are all over the place! Some sellers only
use whole dollar amounts, some end all of their products in .99,
and some will use multiples of .10 or .25 in all pricing. There are
not significant pros and cons for any format, but *don't mix* pricing
formats. Mixing formats looks unprofessional and messy. Pick
one, and go with it.

It's both appropriate and wise to start a price low and raise it
over time. Reflect on how much you would (fairly!) pay for a new
product you created if you were a buyer, and then list that product for 20% less. When you have several sales of that resource,
and you have received positive ratings and comments, that's a
good indication that it's time to raise the price. At that point, raise
it up to the fair price you originally determined you would pay
for it. After you earn more sales, positive ratings, and reviews,
raise it again.

The price changing process doesn't have to be complicated.
TpT automatically tracks your product statistics, and it's simple to
view how many times each product has sold, what the product's
conversion rate is (i.e., how many *buy* the item after *viewing* the
product page), and what you have earned from that product. I
recommend reviewing these statistics once a year, and for sellers
who are full-time teachers, summer provides the perfect opportunity. Use this information to guide your yearly price changes,
if any. To find these tools, click on the carrot next to your store
name at the top of your page. From there, under the Sell category,
select Product Statistics.

22

Make it Official

Uploading Your Products

This chapter is TpT-specific. Thus far, we have delved deep into the hows and whys of the online curriculum store process, the behind-the-scenes work that makes stores successful. Now it's time to walk through uploading more closely. What happens when you click that little "Upload New Product" button? Have the TpT website up as you look at these uploading sections:

♦ **Product Name and Description.** See the section titled: **Customer Service Strategy #1: Playing Offense.**

♦ **Files.** For the product file, you can click and select your file, or you can drag and drop. You may or may not want to upload a Preview File. TpT has FAQ resources about the difference between a Preview File and a Thumbnail File. You need a Main cover (Thumbnails of your product are optional), and TpT will either auto generate this if the file type is compatible or you can upload your own. For ideas on uploading your own, see the section **Sales Strategy #4: Establishing Curb Appeal**.

♦ **Price.** If this is a free item, select Free Resource. Otherwise, set your price. TpT automatically sets multiple licensing discounts at 10% of the regular price. This seems far too low to me. I like to set my multiple licenses at 50% of the regular price to encourage the multiple licenses to be bought. The Bundle Discount Price is optional.

◆ **Tax code.** You can read the descriptions in the link TpT supplies (it's a pop-up), but most of what teachers upload falls under Digital Images Streaming/Electronic Download.

◆ **Grade level.** Choose up to four grades or select "Not Grade Specific."

◆ **Subject area.** Select up to three subject areas. Remember to select the general "World Language" area if it is a template that anyone teaching World Language could use plus your language *plus* at least one other language.

◆ **Resource type.** Select up to three resource types (e.g., Activity, Game, Assessment, Homework, etc.).

◆ **Custom category.** This relates back to the custom categories you set up in Section 1 (**Get Organized: Setting Your Preliminary Categories**). Products can fit into more than one category.

◆ **Education standards.** This section is entirely optional, and it is always evolving to include sections for individual states' standards.

◆ **Teaching duration.** This is optional. I do not often include anything in this field because I find it too rigid. Instead, I like my product descriptions to include how long I *envision* this product taking in class.

◆ **Total number of pages or slides.** This is optional, but it can be helpful for buyers.

◆ **Answer key.** This is optional. If it doesn't apply because the product is an informational handout, for example, then select "Does Not Apply." But if your product *does* come with an answer key, I recommend checking "Included" here and spelling that out in the product description (e.g., "This product comes with an answer key for the teacher").

◆ **Copyright.** Select one choice to indicate legal compliance.

◆ **Make product active.** The website auto generates to check this bubble, but some sellers might uncheck it if they're still doing revisions on a product and plan to upload it later.

23

Customer Service Strategy #2

Playing Defense

Let's start with a refresher from a previous section:

Customer service is:
50% preventative work
48% engaging with customers
2% dealing with unhappy customers

The 50% that is preventative is the curriculum store equivalent of playing offense; it's writing detailed and honest product descriptions combined with creating clear and creative or practical products. Depending on the product, it may also include adding extra instructions for the teacher and/or input on possible variations for the product. The other 50% is the curriculum store equivalent of playing defense. I cannot stress this enough: a strong offense will limit unpleasant tasks (i.e., dealing with unhappy customers) to no more than 2% of your customer service–related time. That said, even the *strongest* offense will still have unhappy customers. Even the Chicago Bulls' dynasty in the 90s didn't go undefeated!

The 48% of customer service that is engaging with your customers is usually rather simple. Customers can use the Q&A section to ask questions about products before purchasing. We want this! It's much better that buyers ask questions about products to determine if it's right for them than they buy the product, discover it's not what they thought it was, and leave a negative review. Alternatively, sometimes the buyer has already bought the item but they need clarification or have a comment about an issue. The Q&A section will often attract questions such as these:

◆ Would this bundle be appropriate for distance learning?
◆ I found a typo on page 3. Could you fix it and repost? (Note: once a buyer has purchased a product, they continually have access to that product's edits. Each time you edit a product and repost, there is a box you can check to notify your buyers that there was an edit.) This box is located underneath the Product File space.
◆ I thought I was buying a Schoology collection, but I don't see a code. Is there one?
◆ I only have Google docs, not access to Microsoft Office. Is there a way to get this PowerPoint to function fully as a Google doc?
◆ Does this subjunctive activity include irregular verbs?

Fortunately, these questions are usually quick to reply to. To the greatest extent possible, make an effort to reply within 24 hours. An additional step is to ask yourself if other buyers will have the same question. If so, you might have to adjust the products or product descriptions of that item and of related items accordingly.

Sellers also see comments come in when buyers leave positive ratings and reviews. These are encouraging, and they help fuel our little CEO endeavors forward! Some sellers make it a point to reply to each and every positive comment, some never reply, and, of course, there are those who camp out in the middle. Choose what's best for you based on the time you have to devote to customer service versus product creation (because it's still a numbers game!) See Table 23.1 for ideas.

Engaging with customers also includes messaging your followers. The TpT platform allows sellers to message followers once a month, though many do not do it as often as TpT permits.

To find this option, click on the carrot next to your store name at the top of your page. From there, under the Communication category, select Note to Followers. See tips in Table 23.2.

TABLE 23.1

POSITIVE COMMENTS	POSSIBLE REPLIES
Thank you for this wonderful product!	*De rien/De nada/Bitte/Prego/Afwan!*
This is a great, competitive practice/review.	*Merci/Gracias/Danke/Grazie/Shukraan!*
This saved me so much time!	That's awesome to hear!
My students LOVE this game! With this product, I feel like they're really learning something too!	I'm so glad your students enjoyed it! I appreciate the feedback.
Great resource for solidifying the concepts and getting students talking to each other!	Thank you for your business, and have a great rest of the semester!
This product saved me in a pinch! I have bought all of the products in this line, and I can't wait for you to make more!	I'm working on some new products in this line now. Please comment in the Q&A section with specific topics you'd like addressed in this product line, and I'll get to those first. Thank you!

TABLE 23.2

WHY MESSAGE FOLLOWERS	DON'T FORGET TO INCLUDE
◆ You have a new product or product line.	◆ Thank them for their business.
◆ You have a free product that would be useful and/or timely.	◆ Hyperlinks to products in your store.
◆ You're going to throw a sale (more on sales in Section 3).	◆ Wish them a great semester/break/summer/etc.
◆ You're making a change in your store and/or products that you want your customers to be aware of.	◆ Hyperlinks to your blog or YouTube channel

Then there's the remaining 2% of customer service...This is the 2% of customers who will make you want to scream, pull your hair out, and potentially even yell profanities (in multiple languages) at the computer screen. I've been there. We all have. There is nothing you can do to fully prevent this from happening. Much like irrational parents at school, every seller has irrational buyers.

Some sellers choose not to reply to negative comments, and while I understand the "I'm just going to politely walk away so I don't say something I regret" approach, I don't advise it. Negative comments are on your product page for future buyers to see. If you let the negative comment go unchecked, it could deter a future buyer from purchasing your product. Conversely, if you handle customer service in a way that is appropriate and professional, a future buyer may notice, and it might alleviate any fears they had about buying your product after reading the negative review. That said, it's often best to wait 24 hours before replying to a negative review. Cooling down first is a strategic (and smart) move!

If a situation is bad enough, you can report buyers to TpT. TpT will only delete negative comments if they fall into one of three categories:

1. Focus on technical issues (downloading errors, software issues, etc.)
2. Contain abusive or inappropriate language
3. Spam a product's feedback section

Unfortunately, most negative comments don't fall into one of those categories—they're just irrational. Table 23.3 shows actual comments either I received or sellers I know received.

Customers are the component of our business that we can't control. With proper planning and execution, we can take out some of the element of surprise from customer service, and our business will be better for it.

TABLE 23.3

NEGATIVE COMMENTS (altered slightly to preserve anonymity)	POSSIBLE REPLIES
This had a typo.	Thank you for the heads-up! I've fixed it and reposted. Any time you find a typo or mistake, please post on my Q&A wall so I can fix it and repost for everyone.
This product has so many mistakes; it's unusable!	It has been checked by a team and verified by native speakers. It may seem like ___ is a typo, but remember the rule about …
I was expecting something with two columns and examples in Japanese on both sides and…and…	It sounds like you had a specific image in mind when you purchased this… and that sounds like a really cool product! But it does not match the product description that I posted. In the future, please read the product descriptions carefully before making a purchase, and rate the product only according to what it claims to be in the description.
I would prefer that the interrogatives activities not use *cuál* with nouns.	I understand. This is a geographical preference, not a correct/incorrect usage. Fortunately, the product is editable, so you can change that to fit your stylistic preference.
I couldn't download this.	Sounds like a technical glitch. When that happens, please either click on the TpT help button or post on the Q&A wall so I can fix it for you.
I couldn't download this. (This is a common one… hence listing it twice.)	Sounds like a technical glitch, and I understand how frustrating that can be! I looked into it, and everything downloads and opens fine on my end on both a Mac and a PC. So let's try this: Please email me at ____@____ and I'll email you the file. For your inconvenience, if there's anything you'd like in my store that is $____ or under, let me know, and I'll send you that product for free as well.
I really need this quiz! Can I get it for free?	I understand your need, but please understand that this is my business. I do my best to keep prices fair, and I also routinely upload new free items. This quiz, however, is not one of them.
This entire document was in GERMAN!	I am sorry you did not get what you were looking for. My store name is in German, my products are in German, my bio says I teach German, and this product was tagged "German." If there is a way I could make it more clear for buyers in the future, please let me know, and I would be happy to change it. It is my goal to provide clear and accurate product descriptions, and I'm sorry that was not the case in this instance.
I could've made this.	There are very few items on TpT that we can't all make—there are so many talented teachers out there! I try to be clear in my product descriptions so there are no surprises, but if there's something I can add, please let me know, and I'd be happy to make the description more clear.

WORKSPACE

Customer Service Goals and Brainstorming

What do I need to add to my
current product descriptions to
proactively avoid negative reviews?

-
-
-
-

By when will I accomplish those
product description changes?

(Now put it in your calendar!)

How often will I message followers?

When will be my first message?

(Now put it in your calendar!)

What will I include in my messages
to followers?

-
-
-

To what extent will I interact with
customers? When will I reply?

-
-
-

How will I prevent a bad rating/
comment?

-
-
-

24

Data Collection

Tracking Your Progress

Tracking the growth of our online store is useful, and it's a lot of fun when we see upward-moving trends! As a teacher, we generally trade time for money. As a curriculum seller, however, we have fantastic potential for passive income. Basically, that means that we can make money while we sleep!

Although the very first item you ever upload can still make you money ten or more years down the line, there may be a point where your store's progress levels off somewhat. This is typically due, in large part, to a leveling off of *product uploads*, so remember the Golden Rule for Selling:

It's a numbers game.

Tracking your sales, products, and followers is a wise and simple practice for sellers. You can set this up in an Excel document or a Google Sheet, or even a basic notebook will do. I recommend tracking monthly earnings, yearly earnings, the number of products in your store, the number of followers you have, and the percentage increases from year to year. See Table 24.1.

Knowing and anticipating trends can also help your metrics when you notice those lulls in growth. Trends are an excellent guide for when to ramp up product creation and posting and when to sit back and take a breather. See Table 24.2.

TABLE 24.1

	Year 1	Year 2	% Increase	Year 3	% Increase
January Earnings					
February					
March					
April					
May					
June					
July					
August					
September					
October					
November					
December					
Total Yearly Earnings					
# of Products in Store					
# of Followers					

TABLE 24.2

TYPICALLY HIGH SALES	TYPICALLY LOW SALES (Budget for this!)
◆ Right before a major holiday. (This could be of the seller's home country or a TL country.) ◆ Right before a school break ◆ Back-to-school rush ◆ Second semester (nearly all of it!) ◆ Sunday (all day) though Wednesday morning	◆ June ◆ July ◆ December, May, and August are more or less "half months" for TpT sales ◆ Winter break ◆ Wednesday afternoon through Saturday

Lastly, TpT (and other platforms) have excellent tools for tracking various metrics. In TpT, your seller dashboard is full of valuable data. There, you can track your sales and earnings for whatever date range you choose. To do this, click on the carrot next to your store name at the top of your page. Under the Sell category, select Dashboard.

You can also track your store's traffic or, in other words, how buyers got to your store. The Traffic tab is next to the Dashboard tab.

There is a Marketing tab that links to different resources for sellers to market their resources. Some sellers use these extensively, while some don't use them at all. The Marketing tab is next to the Traffic tab.

A simple tool you can use to look at individual products is the Product Statistics area. There, you can check the conversion rate of each product (i.e., how many buyers *purchase* the resource after *viewing* it,) how many times the product has sold, how much money in sales the product has generated, how much money the product has generated in earnings for the seller, and more. To find the Product Statistics area, click on the carrot next to your store name at the top of your page. Under the Sell category, select Product Statistics.

Looking at metrics can be overwhelming, so when you're just starting out with your store, I recommend putting metrics on the back burner. The great thing about them is that you don't have to *do* anything to keep them going—they're automatic. So whenever you're ready to dive in, all of the information will be saved there for you.

Section 2 Homework

It's time to fill up your store! Here is a checklist of items to complete:

♦ Create products
  ◊ Products should be clear and creative or clear and practical.
  ◊ Include answer keys.
  ◊ Make products editable.
  ◊ If you already have items in your store, change what you need to make them editable and include answer keys.
♦ Upload products
  ◊ Establish "curb appeal."
  ◊ Write clear and honest descriptions.
♦ Spend time researching other sellers
  ◊ What trends do you notice for products?
  ◊ What holes (opportunities!) do you see for products?
  ◊ What do you notice with pricing?
♦ Create bundles and super bundles
♦ Hyperlink products to other products in your store
♦ Make templates
♦ Create a data tracking sheet
♦ Take another look at your categories. Are there any you need to change? Any to add?
♦ Complete the workspace pages

Look at you go! You are filling up your store with quality products that will help other teachers and students while simultaneously earning you income. This is a huge feat, and you deserve some time off. Maybe you'd like to reward yourself with something fun, perhaps?

In Section 3, we focus on creating a successful online store. Here, we look at "leveling up," and diving deeper into nuances, extras, possibilities, and related information. Some of the ideas will speak to you and your skill set, and some won't. That's okay! The goal is growth, however you want to achieve it.

SECTION 3
Growing a Successful Store

25

Opening Thoughts

You opened a store, you filled it with some of the best products you created, and you started making money! Awesome! At some point you'll hit autopilot, and you may wonder, "What's my next step?" This section covers several of those "next steps," but I want to stress that you don't *have* to get to all of them. This is *your* curriculum store, and *you* are the only person who knows how you want to run it, what kind of time you have to devote to it, and what you hope it will do for you.

Remember in Section 1 when you read that all buyers aren't you? Well, all sellers aren't you either. There are nearly as many kinds of sellers on the curriculum platforms as there are buyers, and every seller operates differently. Some sellers will disagree with the "next steps" in this section, arguing that some of these steps should be done from the beginning. Other sellers won't *ever* do some of these steps, and still others yet will argue that there are key steps missing. Some might start an online store with the goal of getting a little side income—maybe $100 per month—but there are also sellers for whom online curriculum selling is their *full-time job*.

Every seller is different.
Every store is different.

The basic message is this: as long as you operate ethically, do what works best for you in the situation you're in at the time.

26

Crystal Clear

Creating Your Terms of Use

There's a famous exchange in the classic movie *A Few Good Men* between Jack Nicholson's character (a rather intense Marine colonel) and Tom Cruise's character (a young military lawyer) during a murder trial:

> *Jack:* "Are we clear?"
> *Tom:* "Yes, sir."
> *Jack (louder, angrier):* "ARE WE CLEAR?"
> *Tom:* "Crystal."

Crystal-like clarity is what we want for our customers. We already covered some of this with product descriptions, but another step in establishing clarity happens in your Terms of Use (TOU) or User Agreement page.

Simply put, the TOU page goes with every product you sell, and its job is to outline exactly what the purchase of this product does and doesn't allow the buyer to do with it. I highly recommend searching online and checking out different TOU pages to see what others include, but Table 26.1 has some ideas.

You may also choose to include any of the following information on the TOU page:

TABLE 26.1

WHAT YOU CAN DO WITH THIS PRODUCT	WHAT YOU CANNOT DO WITH THIS PRODUCT
◆ Use it for personal use ◆ Use it in your classroom with your students ◆ Make copies for your students ◆ Alter it to suit your needs in your classroom ◆ Professionally reference it (in a blog, presentation, speech, etc.), provided credit is given to me and my online store ◆ Share it on your school's specific learning platform for use/view by your students only	◆ Allow other teachers to use it ◆ Allow its use in classrooms/with students who are not your own ◆ Claim it as your own ◆ Resell it ◆ Alter it and resell it ◆ Distribute it for free by any means ◆ Post the document online ◆ Remove the copyright info ◆ Post it online where anyone can download/use it

- ◆ a "thank you for your purchase" statement
- ◆ your store logo
- ◆ your store's social media info
- ◆ your blog URL
- ◆ Intellectual Property (IP) lawyer's info

Some sellers absolutely argue that you need a TOU page from Day 1…but if you are (or have been) a buyer on an online school resource platform, you know that not everyone includes a TOU page. Your store can absolutely function without one, but I do think it's an important, easy-to-make document. So while I'm calling it a "next step" because you don't *need* one, I'm also listing it *first* because I think it's the most important.

27

Everyone Loves a Discount

Throwing Sales

Throwing a sale in your store is an easy way to attract and retain customers. If you use TpT as your platform, the TpT website is set up for you to easily manage this through their built-in tools. There are three primary ways to have a sale in your store or give a discount:

1. **TpT site-wide sales**

    TpT hosts site-sponsored sales a few times each year (e.g., Back to School), which provide a great opportunity for sellers to get on board. Once logged into your account, you'll see a banner notifying you of the upcoming sale. It will say something like: *Hello Teacher-Author! Our [name] sale is coming up on [date]. Ready your store.*

    When you click on "Ready your store" (or, alternatively, Home -> Dashboard -> Throw a Sale) you will have two options: TpT allows teacher-authors to set their own sale parameters, or they can also opt to simply place everything in their store at 20% off.

    If you set your own sale info, your discount options are 5%, 10%, 15%, and 20%, and you can choose whether you want it to be every item in your store or only certain products.

2. **Individual store sales**

You also have the ability to throw sales (using the same process) any time you'd like, though TpT recommends no more than once per month. Throw a Sale is under the Promote area of your store's Dashboard (carrot by your store name.)

You can choose to promote these sales with messages to followers, or you can use them as "secret" sales where the only way buyers would know about them is by visiting your store during the sale. It depends how much time and work you want to put into it!

3. **"Unofficial" sales**

Unofficial sales are useful tools to engage with your followers. They are particularly handy if you have a new product or product line that you want to highlight. Let's say a particular new product will sell for $3.00. You can message your followers something like this: "Hello, fellow Japanese teacher followers! I am excited about a new product in my store: <u>Guide to Making Fun and Easy Sushi at Home</u>. This item consists of handouts and a step-by-step video for students and families. The regular price is $3.00, but for a limited time only, it is just $1.00! This surprise sale is advertised only to my followers as a thank you for your business, and it lasts from ____ through ____. On ____, the price will go back up to $3.00, so get it while you can!"

Additionally, you can use unofficial sales as a reward for good customers or as a way to "play defense" with unhappy customers. In either situation, you can ask the customer (via the Comments or Q&A sections they used to communicate with you) to contact you on your TpT-linked email, and let them know that your store will be on sale for them for a specific period of time. I recommend doing this for no more than one to two hours at a time. TpT doesn't allow you to set times—only dates—so to make this work you have to do it a semi-manually. Agree on a start time with the buyer, and go through the TpT-site steps of a one-day sale. At the end of the time you allowed your buyer, or after you see that buyer made their purchase, simply delete/end the sale manually.

As always, each seller operates differently. You can choose to do sales every month, only stick to the TpT site-wide sales, not ever do sales, or anything in between.

WORKSPACE

Sales

When will I throw my first sale?   (Now put it in your calendar!)

How often will I throw a sale?   (Now put a couple dates in your calendar!)

What percentage discount will my sales be?

28

Refine Your Entrepreneurial Skills

Creating a Product Line

Although creating a product line technically is about *filling* your store, it's more likely that during the initial process of filling your store you're a little bit all over the place…and that's okay! It's not necessary to have a road map from the get-go, and it so often happens in the beginning that we have ideas from here to there that we run after until we get distracted by another one.

But after the dust settles, we take a look in our store, and we try to make sense of what's there and, more importantly, what's missing. At that point, it's time to sit back and consider what opportunities you have for product lines. Likely, you already have some product lines started, but you may not have called them that yet. Product lines can start in one of two primary ways:

1. You start with areas of content for which you create resources.
2. You start with a list of resources you're skilled at creating.

Let's dissect each of those approaches.

In the first approach, we start with areas of content and branch out. I think it's easiest to sort these into three primary areas: vocabulary content, grammar content, cultural content. Vocabulary might encompass themes such as "family" or "travel," or it might be more precise like "numbers." Grammar content might include specific tenses and verbs as well as discrete topics such as pronoun usage. Cultural content is pretty open, so here you can refer back to the workspace in the chapter about culture to see what cultural concepts you cover. When sifting through this material, make an actual *list* of your content areas. (Yes, write them down.)

Once you lay out your areas of content, then consider your resources. For example, perhaps you have a game you created that you love and that you think is good for kids. We'll call it "Bamboozled" (because why not?) To create a product line, you'll go through each and every area of content on your list and make a Bamboozled game to fit that topic: –AR Verb Bamboozled Game, Pronoun Bamboozled Game, Subjunctive Formation Bamboozled Game, Latin American Countries Bamboozled Game, etc. *Voilà!* There's your product line!

The second approach is the opposite of the first. In the second approach, you start by listing (physically listing, on paper) each of your products that you feel are strong because they are clear, practical, and/or creative. These are the products that make you think, "Yes! Kids will benefit from this! This will help kids learn the language!" Here, you might have the Bamboozled Game, a WebQuest activity, and a speaking and writing partner activity you call "Chat & Scribble," among others.

When the list of your top products is complete, then you consider areas of content that would best match your products. What are all the areas where Bamboozled fits? Create Bamboozled games for each of those topics. What are all the areas where a WebQuest is applicable? Create WebQuests for each area. What topics could work for Chat & Scribble activities? Create Chat & Scribbles for all of those topics. Check! Product line complete!

As you create and upload one product at a time, you may find it useful to send a message to your followers, alerting them to the product line creation. You can include hyperlinks to the products that are already uploaded as well as give them a sneak peek of what's coming next and when they can expect to see those resources in the store. Additionally, when you're first announcing a new product line to your followers, it can be enticing to potential buyers if a sale came with it.

	A	B Game 1	C Game 2	D Game 3	E Partner Activity 1	F Partner Activity 2	G Partner Activity 3	H Quiz style 1	I Quiz style 2	J Speaking activity	K Writing Activity	L Reading Activity	M Listening Activity
2	Topic 1	X	X	X	X	X	X	X	X		X	X	X
3	Topic 2		X	X	X	X	X	X	X			X	X
4	Topic 3	X	X	X	X	X		X	X		X	X	
5	Topic 4	X	X	X	X	X	X	X	X	X	X	X	X
6	Topic 5	X	X	X	X	X	X	X	X		X	X	X
7	Topic 6	X	X	X		X	X	X	X		X	X	X
8	Topic 7	X	X	X	X	X	X	X	X		X	X	X
9	Topic 8	X	X	X	X	X	X	X	X		X	X	X
10	Topic 9	X	X	X	X	X	X	X	X		X	X	X
11	Topic 10	X		X	X	X	X	X	X		X	X	X

FIGURE 28.1 Sample Product Line Tracking Sheet

Don't forget to wrap up your product line with a strong finish! Once you have created an entire product line, of course, it's time to create a bundle: "Mega Pack of 15 Bamboozled Games for Arabic Learners!" It is helpful to potential buyers if your product lines (including the bundles) have visual continuity as well. They all could use the same graphic as the main cover or, even more simply, you might use the same PowerPoint slide design as the main cover. Whatever your choice, find a way to let buyers see your product line exists before they even read any words.

You may want to create an organizational chart such as the one in Figure 28.1 to track your product lines.

29

The Pied Piper

Garnering Followers

Some sellers go after followers like Simone Biles goes after gold medals. They're *intense*! For example, sellers such as these will routinely look for new sellers on the platform, personally message them, and ask them for a "follow." In return, they say they will follow the new seller's store.

I am not one of those sellers. First of all, I don't have that kind of time, but I also (personally) find it a little too much. For me, it's akin to stepping into a store and immediately having the sales associate try to bring me 50 different items. I think, "I'm not interested, actually, and I kind of just want to look on my own." My personal philosophy is to let followers happen naturally. To me, positive reviews affect my sales significantly more than my number of followers.

But sellers are all different, right? You may decide that this or a similar approach works for you, in which case, go for it! An appropriate place to start might be with all of your friends and/ or colleagues whom you know have their own stores. A message of "Hey, want to follow each other?" will likely be met with a "Sure! What's your store name?"

If your take is to be more passive about attracting followers, simply take care to make your store name and brand known. This might mean:

- ◆ adding it to your business cards
- ◆ putting it in your (personal) email signature
- ◆ attaching it to slides for conferences at which you present
- ◆ tagging/hyperlinking your store in social media posts
- ◆ adding a specific message to your store banner (info on TpT's site) such as: *Follow my store to receive announcements about sales and flash freebies!*
- ◆ posting products that give the buyer a sense that they might want to stay in touch (e.g., a "growing bundle" quote so the buyer wants to receive alerts about product updates)

 WORKSPACE

Reflect on the idea of followers and what your personal comfort and skill levels are regarding obtaining them. Put a check under the appropriate answer.

	This would work for me.	It's a "maybe..."	This isn't me at all.
I can directly message store owners of my same target language to ask them to follow me and follow them in return.			
I can directly ask friends and colleagues who teach my target language to follow my store.			
I can put a link to my store in my email signature.			
I can promote my store and ask for followers via my social media.			
I can put my store on my business cards.			
I can attach a promotional slide for my store to presentations I give.			
I can put a banner in my store that tells buyers to follow my store for flash sales and new product announcements.			

30

Teamwork Makes the Dream Work

Working with a Partner

World Language teachers are in a unique position to create a "seller team": a duo or small group of sellers who work together to boost each other's sales potential.

For example, let's say that you teach French, and your friend teaches Spanish. You created games A, B, and C that you particularly like and find creative; your colleague has done the same with her games X, Y, and Z. You both have done well in your respective stores with your games, and you are looking to expand your store with new product lines. You can each create templates for your games (in English), share them with each other, and give each other written permission to use the templates. Then you each will take the other's games, translate them into your target language, fit them to topics of your choice, and sell them in your store. *Voilà*! You now have brand new product lines!

Although partnerships work best if you teach different languages, it can also work if you teach the same language. Here are a few ideas:

1. You write all of your products together, split the cost of a premium membership, and split monthly sales. The downside here is that you have to carve out a time to work together that fits both of your schedules.

2. Your store is expressly for lower levels, and your partner's store is expressly for upper levels. You create products A, B, and C for lower levels and then hand them over to your partner. Your partner then creates the upper-level versions of those products and posts them in his or her store. Of course, this works in reverse as well. Here, your stores function as "sister stores," and you can even market them together that way. This strategy works well if you don't have a lot of time to dedicate to your store because you'll have a partner doing a significant share of the work. The downside is that it's useful to create a requirement of sorts for the work you each create. For example: "By the end of the month, we will have each created ten resources and handed them over to each other." That way, it keeps the workload fair, and it helps to prevent frustration.

3. You and your partner make a list of themes that you want to cover in your stores (e.g., family, school, travel, activities). Then you divide the list in two; your store will focus on the first half of the list, and your partner's store will focus on the second half. Whenever you make a resource, you hand it over to your partner, to whom you then give permission to tailor that resource to fit his or her themes. Your partner will do the same. This strategy also works well if you don't have a lot of time to dedicate to a store, and it's another example of a situation in which it's important to have a working agreement with your partner.

Though I, personally, strongly believe in the partnership strategy, it's not for everyone. It's vital that you and your seller partner are of a similar mindset. Are your work habits compatible? Are you similarly organized? Do you have a comparable approach to your business? If the answers to those questions are "Yes," then this might be a winning strategy for you!

An additional bonus of a partnership is that you and your partner could hire the same IP lawyer and navigate legal issues together. Once an IP lawyer becomes familiar with online curriculum platforms, he or she can explain it faster to the next person, which saves money for everyone.

Another benefit is having a partner to cheer you along, push you when you need it, and provide feedback for ideas. This can be particularly valuable when you're low on inspiration or motivation. Sometimes simply hearing about what my seller partner is creating gives me energy to tackle some of my own To Do list for my store! My partner and I also will periodically share feedback we receive from buyers with each other and ask how the other would respond. It's a lot easier to respond to a negative review when we have worked through it with someone else first.

If you do choose to work in any level of partnership, a word of caution: it's dangerous to compare. The two (or more) of you are not in competition with each other; you are there to support each other. Using the example above, someone may think, "Well, if the French teacher gives the Spanish teacher activities A, B, and C, the Spanish teacher could make a lot more money off those products than the French teacher could because there is a bigger base of Spanish teacher buyers." This may be true in the United States, but what is also true is that an American Spanish teacher also has more *competition* (in the form of other Spanish teacher sellers on curriculum platforms) than a French teacher does. This is only one example, but my point is that if you're going to nitpick, a partnership isn't the right way to go.

💭 **WORKSPACE**

Establishing a Team

Who might be a potential partner?	What can I share with my colleague(s)?	What could my colleague(s) share?
• -----------------------	• -----------------------	• -----------------------
	-----------------------	-----------------------
	-----------------------	-----------------------
	-----------------------	-----------------------
• -----------------------	• -----------------------	• -----------------------
	-----------------------	-----------------------
	-----------------------	-----------------------
	-----------------------	-----------------------
• -----------------------	• -----------------------	• -----------------------
	-----------------------	-----------------------
	-----------------------	-----------------------
	-----------------------	-----------------------
• -----------------------	• -----------------------	• -----------------------
	-----------------------	-----------------------
	-----------------------	-----------------------
	-----------------------	-----------------------
• -----------------------	• -----------------------	• -----------------------
	-----------------------	-----------------------
	-----------------------	-----------------------
	-----------------------	-----------------------

31

More Screen Time

Leveraging Social Media and Other Tech Options

The words "social media" tend to elicit strong reactions. People either get excited and think engaging and using social media is fun, or they groan and share how the best month ever was the month they took a break from all social media. Love it or hate it, leveraging social media remains an *option* for expanding your curriculum store's reach.

In general, social media can be particularly useful in three areas: advertising, joining a group, and starting a group. The various platforms all offer different forms of free advertising for your store and products, which is an obvious bonus. But in my opinion, the bigger bonus is the opportunity to network and be part of a group. I highly recommend checking out what groups there are out there for your language and/or seller-specific groups for your language. And if there isn't one, start one yourself! Chances are, there are other teacher-authors out there looking for support and camaraderie as well.

Keep in mind that if you want to do social media for your store, you may find it best to create an entirely new account on that platform. Remember, you're a CEO, and you have your own store, which is a *business*. It can be beneficial to keep business and personal largely separate. For more platform-specific ideas, see Table 31.1.

TABLE 31.1

PINTEREST

How to promote your store	**How to network and get ideas**
◆ Pin every item in your store to a board ◆ Make a Pinterest board for each of your curriculum store's categories	◆ Check out what other teacher-authors are pinning

FACEBOOK

How to promote your store	**How to network and get ideas**
◆ Make a business page ◆ Promote sales and new products ◆ Encourage interaction ◆ Give away random freebies	◆ Join seller pages specific to your online platform—there are several! When you find them, check the following before joining: 1. When was the last post? 2. How many messages/posts are there per day? 3. Do you need to request permission to join? 4. Do they prohibit posting sale/product info in their group? (Yes, some do.)

TWITTER

How to promote your store	**How to network and get ideas**
◆ Create a business account ◆ Tweet about sales and new products ◆ Retweet related info	◆ Follow others' handles (in the hopes that they'll follow you) ◆ Follow your selling platform ◆ Follow trends (hashtags) that relate to your language, teaching, or a specific style of teaching (e.g., TPRS)

INSTAGRAM

How to promote your store	**How to network and get ideas**
◆ Create a business account ◆ Post photos of your classroom ◆ Post photos of projects created by you (not students—FERPA!)	◆ Check out what other teacher-authors are posting ◆ Try to get a product promoted by a teacher-influencer

The Internet and related technologies comprise considerably more than social media platforms though. So what else could be a next step for you? How else could you expand your business in different, yet related ways?

◆ **Download the app for your curriculum platform.** The TpT app is free, for example, and it's a great tool for staying more connected to your store. Plus, every time a sale goes through you hear a little "ka-CHING" sound, and that's just fun!

◆ **Start a blog.** Blogging is a cheap way to be actively involved in our profession. You can write about your experience as a teacher, ideas you have for classrooms, or your take on cutting-edge educational research... the options are endless! But what you should certainly include in at least some of your blogs are hyperlinks to items in your online store. You can also effectively use a blog to alert only blog followers to flash sales in your store. Wordpress, Wix, and Square Space all offer free or low-cost blogging and support. With enough followers, you can monetize your blog with Google AdSense and/ or an Amazon affiliate account, for example, and generate advertising and affiliate income.

◆ **Start a YouTube channel.** If video production is part of your skill set, it might be time to set up a YouTube channel! Channels associated with online stores are powerful supplements to your store because it gives you a platform to explain your products and show how they work. Like a blog, YouTube can also be monetized. And because YouTube is part of the Google universe, it makes your products searchable, which can bring in teachers (buyers!) who do a search on Google rather than on the selling platform itself.

◆ **Start an email newsletter.** If you have a blog, there are simple plugins you can use to collect email addresses from subscribers. You can then send those contacts a monthly (for example) email that highlights new products, tech tools, news in TL-speaking countries, travel deals, etc.

◆ **Sell on another platform.** There are multiple curriculum resource platforms out there, and there's nothing that says you can't have a store on more than one platform.

◆ **Start your own podcast.** Do you have audio recording skills? Put them to use with a podcast! Personally, my favorite podcasts are short ones—10–15 minutes per episode—so it wouldn't have to be a massive time commitment. You could establish a podcast that covers World Language news and strategies in general or one that specifically is for teachers of your target language.

If you're thinking about a blog or a YouTube Channel as potential steps for you, this is where language choice comes back into play. If you choose to have a store name (blog, YouTube Channel, podcast...) that is not in English, it's especially important to choose one without special characters or accents, as you cannot use those in the URL. Additionally, the use of special characters can make it harder for other teachers to find your platforms.

TABLE 31.2

WORKSPACE
What are my tech-related options?

Option	Am I interested in this?		Do I already have a skill set for this, or would I have to learn first?	
Pinterest	Yes	No	Already have	Need to learn
Facebook	Yes	No	Already have	Need to learn
Twitter	Yes	No	Already have	Need to learn
Instagram	Yes	No	Already have	Need to learn
App for selling platform	Yes	No	Already have	Need to learn
Blog	Yes	No	Already have	Need to learn
YouTube channel	Yes	No	Already have	Need to learn
Newsletter	Yes	No	Already have	Need to learn
Store on another platform	Yes	No	Already have	Need to learn
Start a podcast	Yes	No	Already have	Need to learn

32

Menu of Options

Considering Related Possibilities

For most sellers, the "leveling up" step happens after you've had your store open for a while. You've filled (and filled...and filled...) your store with products, and you've hit a plateau. It's the time when you're thinking, "What can I do *now*? What comes *next*?" First, consider ideas we've previously discussed:

♦ Do you have an IP lawyer? If not, maybe now is the right time to hire one.
♦ Do you have a logo you like? If not, maybe it's time to check on fiverr.com or to talk to artists in your network.
♦ Is your store an LLC? If you're interested in that route, now could be a good time.
♦ Have you made templates?
♦ Have you made bundles, big and small?
♦ Have you included TOU pages with all of your products?
♦ Have you found a colleague/friend with whom you could partner?

Then again, it's possible that you have either gone through those steps or you're not interested in them. Fair enough. Although certainly not exhaustive, here's a list of other ideas for "next steps":

◆ **Get business cards.** There seems to *always* be a Groupon for cheap business cards through common printing services.

◆ **Get a business bank account.** Especially if you have an LLC, a business account is essential for keeping personal and business earnings separate.

◆ **Present at a conference.** No, this doesn't have to be about online curriculum selling. Present on your topic of expertise, but make sure each teacher in the audience receives your business card...you know, the one with your store info!

◆ **Watermark your products.** Some sellers watermark from Day 1, and others never do. It's especially helpful for Preview Images, if you use them.

◆ **Teach a class to other teachers.** Again, this doesn't have to be about online curriculum sales. It could be a class taught through your local union, or maybe it's a community education class for teachers, but either way, make sure the participants get your business card.

◆ **Email your potential network.** Let's say you have an idea for a brand-new class, but there's no curriculum for it *anywhere*. You have a hunch this class is actually taught around the country (world?) but that teachers who teach it have to create everything on their own. Do a quick Google search for the name of the class, find schools where the class is taught, and email the teachers who teach it. Introduce yourself, and explain that you have resources for them in your online store, which is, of course, hyperlinked in your email signature. (I would throw in a freebie with the email too!)

◆ **Get featured on a podcast.** Is there a podcast related to one of your areas of expertise? Often, podcast hosts are looking for interviewees, and you might be just what they're looking for! When the host introduces you, he or she can give a shout-out to your online store, as well as put a link to it in the show notes.

◆ **Write a book or an eBook.** Do you have ideas that you think would be useful for World Language teachers?

Write a book! An eBook, in particular, is relatively easy to publish without much help, and with social media it's easier than ever to self-promote. Your eBook or paperback can include information about your online store in it, and if you have print copies of your book you can also sell them in your curriculum store. (Yes, your online store isn't only for digital items! They just happen to be the most popular.)

I cannot stress enough that just because these options are possible doesn't mean you have to do them. Ever. They are just here, sitting in this book, waiting for you *if* the time comes that you toy with the idea of branching out and are looking for some ideas.

WORKSPACE

Leveling Up

Idea	Am I interested in this?	What do I have to do to see this through? Is there someone I should contact?
Hire IP lawyer	Yes No	
New logo	Yes No	
Establish an LLC	Yes No	
Templates	Yes No	
Bundles	Yes No	
TOU page	Yes No	
Business cards	Yes No	
Business bank account	Yes No	
Present at a conference	Yes No	
Watermark products	Yes No	
Teach a class	Yes No	
Email potential buyers	Yes No	
Podcast feature	Yes No	

33

April is Coming

Tackling Tax Time

When tax time comes around, your store income and expenses will play a role. Remember that your store earnings are *taxable income*, and there is an electronic trail to support that. Typically, curriculum store income is a separate Schedule C form for tax reporting, though it is worth noting that precise tax rules and regulations vary from state to state, so always make sure to come to your tax professional with the following.

It's important to remember that both state and federal tax laws regularly change. Keep in touch with your tax professional about these changes, but in the meantime, simply keep a detailed, yearly record of anything you think *might* come up during tax time.

TABLE 33.1

QUESTIONS TO ASK	BRING THIS INFORMATION WITH YOU
◆ Can I deduct the fees I paid to my IP lawyer?	◆ The total you paid for the year in lawyer fees.
◆ Can I deduct all or some of my Internet bill?	◆ The total you paid for the year to your Internet provider.
◆ Can I deduct all or some of my cell phone bill?	◆ The total you paid for the year to your cell phone provider.
◆ Can I deduct fees paid to set up my LLC?	◆ The total you paid to set up an LLC.
◆ Can I deduct fees paid for "extras" such as fonts, software programs, and clip art?	◆ The total you paid for any "extras" you used to create your products.
◆ Can I deduct all or some of the cost of a new computer or cell phone?	◆ The total you paid for a new computer or cell phone that you used for business purposes.
◆ At what point would it be advantageous for me to pay taxes on my store earnings on a quarterly basis? How do I do that? (If you choose to do this, it can be advantageous to set aside a portion of your earnings every month to use for taxes.)	◆ Your total store *sales* for the year *and* your total store *earnings* for the year. (The difference between the two is the commission the platform took, and it may be considered a business expense.)
◆ Can I deduct all or some of the cost of professional development as it relates to education?	◆ Any information from your curriculum store platform's website regarding taxes in your specific state. This information is routinely updated, so it's best to check once a year.

34

Dream Big

Setting Two Types of Goals

The last section of this book is called "Growing a Successful Store." But what is success? More than likely, my idea of success isn't the same as yours; similarly, it is different for each person reading this book. Some of you might want your venture to become your full-time job, and others might just need a creative outlet that utilizes their teaching skill set. Whatever your definition of success is, it all starts with your goals.

Goal setting is one of the most important aspects of your teacher-author journey. I like to look at goals in two different categories:

1. **SMART goals.** You may be familiar with the SMART concept through your teaching, but if not, it's an acronym:
   S = Specific
   M = Measurable
   A = Achievable
   R = Relevant
   T = Time-Based
   As a teacher-author and curriculum seller, you have immediate control over SMART goals.
2. **Milestone goals.** These are goals that we likely don't have a lot of direct control over. We can do things that influence them, yes, but ultimately, it's out of our hands. We also can't set a date by which we will achieve milestone goals.

TABLE 34.1

EXAMPLES OF SMART GOALS (Note: These need a deadline attached to truly be SMART)	EXAMPLES OF MILESTONE GOALS
◆ Create # resources per week/month/year... ◆ Upload # resources per week/month/year... ◆ Work # hours per week/month on your curriculum store ◆ Redo all product covers to create more "curb appeal" ◆ Attach a TOU page to every product ◆ Pin each product in my store to Pinterest ◆ Achieve # total resources in my store	◆ # of followers ◆ # of reviews ◆ Earn $___ per month ◆ Pay for a trip with curriculum store money ◆ Quit my side job because my curriculum store income now makes up for that money ◆ Quit my full-time job and work solely on my curriculum store, allowing me to become location-independent

SMART Goals and Milestone Goals are two sides of the same coin, and I firmly believe in approaching an online curriculum store with a mix of both. Reaching each type of goal constitutes a success, and each success gives us renewed energy to propel us forward in this business venture.

Additionally, you might find value in giving your SMART goals a focus that changes on a yearly basis. Your first year your SMART goals might focus on filling your store with products, and there's a precise number of products you're shooting to add each month. Maybe the second year, however, you want to shift your focus to earning more followers, so you create SMART goals that support that focus. The third year, perhaps your focus is new products and legal compliance. You create a brand-new series of games with product lines to go with them, and you hire a lawyer because the money is flowing! Then the fourth year you shift your focus to culture.

Your first step is to use the following workspace to write down SMART and Milestone Goals that you currently have for yourself and/or your store. Remember to also put the deadline for each of your SMART Goals in your planner, online calendar, or on a notepad that you often reference—anywhere you'll have a reminder! The second step is to revisit these concepts and make *new* goals as you meet each previous goal and your journey continues.

WORKSPACE

SMART Goals & Milestone Goals

SMART goal = something you can control; an accomplishment of preset parameters

SMART = Specific, Measurable, Achievable, Relevant, Time-Based

Write down SMART goals that you have for your curriculum store. What are the things that will help you feel like you're getting somewhere and encourage you to do more? Start small, and then go big!

Milestone goal = something you have little control over; something you reach *during your process*

Write down milestone goals that you want to reach with curriculum store. What metrics might you try to track?

- ---------------------------------

- ---------------------------------

- ---------------------------------

- ---------------------------------

- ---------------------------------

- ---------------------------------

- ---------------------------------

- ---------------------------------

- ---------------------------------

- ---------------------------------

- ---------------------------------

- ---------------------------------

35

Marie Kondo Your World

Staying Organized

Some teacher-authors are gifted organizers. The Container Store is a little slice of Heaven for them, and when Marie Kondo's bestseller *The Life-Changing Magic of Tidying Up* was released they thought, "Finally! Our moment to shine! Now the world will see our worth!" Other teacher-authors are…well…less gifted in that area.

While I can see how some might argue that organization isn't necessary in a "side hustle" type of business and instead opt for a more fly-by-the-seat-of-my-pants approach, I believe it is necessary for the simple reason that we're dealing with money. There is a digital trail of money that you earn and that is filtered to you from the curriculum platform you work with, so to protect yourself, stay organized.

I prefer simple organizational tools, but if you want to go complex, it's your call! To keep all of your store info in one spot, I recommend a basic three-ring binder with four tabbed dividers:

1. **Metrics.** These can be any metrics you choose, but if your goal is to *grow* your store (and, thus, your income,) tracking is key. You might use a chart like the one provided in the Data Collection chapter, or you might decide that there's a better way for you or different data you want to track. This is an easy area to use a Google Sheet or Excel document as well.

2. **Goals.** SMART Goals and Milestone Goals should both be somewhere where you can see them regularly. These serve as inspiration and energy to propel you forward in your business. This is also the space for you to keep track of ideas you have for a yearly *focus* for your goals, if that interests you. If you're more of a visual person, a vision board is an appropriate representation for the Milestone Goals. These images and words could even be the cover of your binder—something to see every time you look at it and a reminder of why you're doing this. "That photo of Thailand is so beautiful! I'm going to do it! I'm going to get there, and my store is going to pay the way! I'm going to create more resources to sell *right now!*"

3. **Taxes.** In this section, keep two items: a list and a plastic document sleeve. The list should comprise all of the questions you have for your tax professional. You'll think of these at random times because different issues will come up as your store grows, so having a place to write them down is a valuable practice. Additionally, the plastic document sleeve is the place where you'll keep receipts of anything that you think *might* be tax-deductible. (On each receipt, I like to highlight the dollar amount.) This way, the receipts are all in one place, and they're easy to grab come tax time. You may also want to keep documentation here of how much you paid in utilities and for your Internet because depending on your home office setup and depending on the tax laws in your state, you might be able to deduct some of those costs.

4. **Ideas.** Especially once you get rolling with your store, see money come in, and track how different resources perform, you'll have ideas for new products all the time! I can say from experience that having Post-it notes in random places is not the best strategy for maximizing content potential!

Of course, everything listed above can absolutely be done digitally. Choose what's right for you, but make sure you have a system in place that supports your goals and makes life easier for growing your store.

Speaking of making life easier, if you teach in a more traditional setting, summer is the perfect time to do a little housekeeping. Try analyzing metrics in the *summer*. Set goals in the *summer*. Print what you need to print (e.g., a data-tracking spreadsheet) in the *summer*. And make sure your store and your plans for it are good to go as you gear up to start the school year.

Organization and general outlook are linked. The more organized we are, the less overwhelmed we're likely to be with our stores. Conversely, the more disorganized we are, the easier it is to become so overwhelmed that we give up all together. You probably now see exactly how many moving parts there are to an online curriculum store...or maybe you saw this all building up several chapters ago. All of the different aspects to consider can absolutely be overwhelming. I get it. Now is probably a good time for a little piece of advice:

Give yourself permission to say "No."

What do I mean by that? Give yourself permission to stick to the basics (whatever that means to you) and to say "No" to anything that doesn't interest you or that you don't currently have time for. It's absolutely okay to say "No" to things you're unsure of because that means you're effectively saying "Yes" to a little bit more sanity!

💭 **WORKSPACE**

Giving Myself Permission

What are the Top Three areas you are giving yourself permission to focus on, exclusively?	What are the Top Three areas you are giving yourself permission to say "No" to for right now, but that you are curious about revisiting later?

1. ---------------------------- 1. ----------------------------

---------------------------- ----------------------------

---------------------------- ----------------------------

---------------------------- ----------------------------

---------------------------- ----------------------------

---------------------------- ----------------------------

---------------------------- ----------------------------

2. ---------------------------- 2. ----------------------------

---------------------------- ----------------------------

---------------------------- ----------------------------

---------------------------- ----------------------------

---------------------------- ----------------------------

---------------------------- ----------------------------

3. ---------------------------- 3. ----------------------------

---------------------------- ----------------------------

---------------------------- ----------------------------

---------------------------- ----------------------------

---------------------------- ----------------------------

---------------------------- ----------------------------

36

Keep On Keepin' On

Finding Inspiration and Staying Motivated

It's a common story: seller starts a store…seller has energy and drive…everything is going well…numbers are going up, up, up… and then…NOTHIN'. No new messages to followers, no new sales, and most of all, no new resources in the store. If this has been you at some point, you're in good company; if this hasn't been you…well, you'll get there.

These tough periods happen for two primary reasons:

1. You've hit a mental block, and you're not sure what to create next. You lack inspiration.
2. You've hit a physical block, and you're not sure you can do any work at all. You lack energy.

So what do you do when it happens? Throw in the towel and abandon your whole professional project all together? Well, you *could*…but I wouldn't recommend it. A side hustle in education is going to ebb and flow for everyone. It's similar to teaching in that way. There are times when we feel absolutely inspired and in sync with our classes, our students, and our curriculum. But there are plenty of other times where we just feel *spent*. And uninspired. And like we're failing. This is echoed in the online curriculum sales world.

Do you lack inspiration? Are you struggling to figure out new materials to create? Here are a few ideas you can come back to when you hit an inspiration roadblock:

◆ **Reread your workspace notes.** Go back through this book and check out your workspace notes. Likely, you will find something that gives you a spark, that makes you think, "Oh, yeah! I forgot about that! I should do that *now!*" Never underestimate how smart and creative an earlier version of yourself was.

◆ **Take a (free) class.** Like many teachers, I geek out about learning. In the movie *Son in Law* Pauly Shore's character had majored in almost everything because he had been in college for so long, and I was jealous of that! If being a full-time student were an occupation, man, sign me up! In the technological age, we have access to limitless classes at the click of a button, and many of these can benefit your business. You can take a class on marketing or on digital design. Or how about "just for fun" classes in your target language? If blogging is interesting to you, you could take a class on setting up a Wordpress (or any other platform) blog. If you're looking for a short class, you can take some classes free of charge on Skill Share, or you can pay a monthly fee for a bigger library of classes. Personally, I'm a huge fan of Massive Open Online Courses (MOOCs), and I love the platforms Coursera.org and EdX.org. I took an *excellent* (and free) course on the French Revolution via Coursera and taught by a professor at the University of Melbourne in Australia. Online courses or local community education courses are all fantastic ways to expand your knowledge base and teach you skills you can use in your business.

◆ **Redesign old materials to fit a new format.** Go through your store's resources with a new lens. *What can I modify so that it is applicable to anyone engaging in distance learning?* With this approach, you're not reinventing the wheel; you're simply modifying an item you already have to fit a different way of teaching and learning.

◆ **Get inspiration from your own favorite things.** Do you have a favorite sport to watch during the Olympics? Do you have a favorite game to play during Game Night with friends or family? Try making a game, activity, or project based on one of those favorites.

◆ **Round out your offerings.** Teaching involves so many different areas: direct instruction, reading, writing, listening, speaking, small group activities, large group activities, projects, assessments, and organizational tools. Take a look at your store and determine which of those areas are well-represented. Which areas might you need to round out a bit more?

But maybe you have ideas; that's not the problem. Is the issue you that you simply don't have energy or drive to work on creating resources? Here are possible solutions you can come back to when you hit an energy roadblock:

◆ **Take a break!** Seriously. Just walk away. You don't have to constantly work on your store in order to be successful. Not by a long shot! In your teaching job you have (or had, if you're no longer teaching) built-in vacation days, so it's important to build in vacation days to your job as a curriculum writer and seller as well. One of the coolest aspects of having a curriculum resource store is that even when you walk away you can still make money! You will still hear that little "ka-CHING" alert from your phone when a purchase goes through, and you'll still get an alert once a month that there is money waiting for you in an account.

◆ **Treat yourself.** There's an endless list of possibilities for what you can do with your store's earnings, but if you haven't done it yet—or if you haven't done it in a while—take a little bit of those earnings and get yourself a "Hey, nice job, You!" treat. It doesn't have to be anything big for it to remind you that there's reward in this hustle. Maybe you get a nice bouquet of flowers for your kitchen table, or maybe you go support your local bookstore and buy a book you've wanted to read. Tickets to a concert or sporting event would be exciting, or a dinner out at a restaurant you've been dying to try could leave you feeling fulfilled and reenergized. Whatever you choose, remind yourself that you earned it.

◆ **Travel.** If you're lacking inspiration and feeling burned out, the absolute most sure-fire cure I know is to travel. You might choose to reenergize yourself by visiting your best friend who lives in another part of the country, or maybe you fly somewhere to check another baseball stadium off your list. Travel *can* just be for fun! But if you're okay with doing a little bit of work while you're gone, and you go to a country that speaks your target language, reread the chapter "Capitalizing on Culture" before you go. The chapter will give you ideas of what to look for and document while you're abroad. This brings up another question for your tax professional: if you're traveling to do work for your store—photos, videos, interviews, etc.— what percentage (if any) of the trip can you write off?

Those are just a few ideas to get you going and give you a jump start in either the inspiration or the energy realm...or both! Ultimately, it doesn't matter what you do. The point is simply to change course in order to find new ideas and renewed enthusiasm. I think you'll find that when allow your store ebb and flow and just *go with it*, the entire journey is more enjoyable.

Section 3 Homework

You have opened an online curriculum store, you have filled it, and you are on a path to growing a successful business. This is huge, and I'm so excited for you! A seller's work is rarely, if ever, done, so here is your To Do List:

- Make a TOU page.
- Plan and throw a sale.
- Set SMART Goals and Milestone Goals.
- Choose any next steps that are appropriate for you...or none at all.
- Go back to previous workspaces to get ideas for resources you can create next.
- Check your metrics
  ◊ What are you selling a lot of? How can you expand that product?
- Buy yourself a (large or small) treat yet with your earnings.

Final Thoughts

Tackling the opening, filling, and growth of a successful curriculum store is a marathon, not a sprint. There will be times when your creative output and your sales are through the roof and other times where you're just "over it." But that's what this book is here for; it's a sort of coach for this process. This book is for you to write in—to be an active participant in the building of your store—and to come back to again and again. One of the most exciting aspects of this business is that there's always something new to try. Each time you come back to your notes in these pages you'll see them in a different light, and they'll give you different ideas.

While it's true that everyone reading this book is, in some ways, in competition with each other, I tend to believe there's room for everyone. Though we are separated by distance, we're still colleagues, and as long as we approach our business ethically, there is no reason we can't support each other. We all have different backgrounds and skill sets, and our stores are avenues for those skills to shine. I wish you the very best of luck in meeting the goals you set for yourself and your business, and should our paths cross someday, please introduce yourself. Until then, keep creating products that are engaging for students and that help teachers around the world. I'm rooting for you!

Printed in the United States
by Baker & Taylor Publisher Services